SILENT SURVIVAL

Finding Myself in the Shadows of a Life I Didn't Choose

LISA LAURENCIO

LANDON
HAIL
PRESS

Paperback ISBN: 978-1-959955-89-4
Hardback ISBN: 978-1-959955-84-9

Published by Landon Hail Press
Book Cover Design by Lisa Laurencio, Rich Johnson, Spectacle Photo
Photo by Jodi Ramos, Millyard Studios

For Ava,
who taught me how to fight, hope, and love
without ever speaking a word

For Desmond and Jillian,
whose love and sacrifices have never gone unnoticed

For Manny,
for his hard work, dedication, and commitment
to providing for our family

Contents

Introduction

I am often asked what my life was like before I had Ava. That question kind of throws me off guard, because I don't ever think about what my life was like back then.

That could be because I tend to be too focused on getting through each day and planning for the days ahead. Or it could be because it causes me to mourn a little bit what once was and what could have been. Maybe the reality is it's a little bit of both.

My life before Ava...? Lisa before Ava? Talk about a throwback. Man, that Lisa, she was a totally different girl. The best way to get to know her would be by starting in my childhood. I don't really have anything bad to say about it. I had a great childhood—a hardworking dad and a loving, hands-on, stay-at-home mom, plus I was very close to my two older brothers. I was a pretty smart kid, had lots of friends, stayed out of trouble (for the most part), and truly loved my life.

For my first thirty-three years of life, right up until I gave birth to Ava, I always got what I wanted. Not in a stuck-up, spoiled-brat kind of way. More like, "If I wanted it and could visualize having it, I got it."

I had a knowing about those kinds of things. I didn't realize it back then, but I had perfected the "let go and let

God" mentality, and I was pretty good at it! I didn't ever hem and haw over anything. If I truly wanted it and could see it happening, I just knew I would get it. On the flip side, if I couldn't picture it, no matter how badly I wanted it or how hard I tried, I simply moved on. It just wasn't for me.

One example of my skills in action happened when I was about ten years old. I was at an event held in our local church's basement, at a Christmas fair. I saw they were running a raffle, and the grand prize was a ten-speed bike. I went over to look at the bike to make sure it was something I really wanted, and I fell in love with it. I could totally visualize tearing up the neighborhood on it, riding over jumps on it, and speeding down the street with my hair blowing in the wind. So, I threw my name into the raffle.

I didn't even bother looking at the other prizes, because I knew, with everything I was, I was going to win that bike. No need to be greedy and try to win more prizes! There was no question in my mind that the bike was mine, and part of me wanted to tell the other kids not to waste their time entering the contest. I mean, they weren't going to win anyway. Good thing I didn't, though, because that would have not attracted any new friends for me or gotten me invited to any cool birthday parties.

Sure enough, two weeks after the raffle closed, the church called to let us know that I won and the bike was mine. This wasn't a one-time incident. This happened over and over again, with anything and everything.

But if I couldn't visualize it, it did not or would not happen. For things from raffles to passing grades on tests to boyfriends, jobs, and even getting married, it didn't matter how much I wanted something. What mattered was if I could actually see myself having it or going through with it.

It helped me to make decisions with total certainty for my entire life. That is, until Ava was born.

I was one of the cliché girly-girls who wanted the sparkly, fairytale wedding gown and big wedding (check), the dark-haired Prince Charming as my groom who swept me off my feet (check), and a little blonde-hair, blue-eyed daughter whom I could dress up like a princess, have tea parties with, bake cookies with, and do all of the special mommy/daughter things. A little mini-me as my instant forever bestie.

So, when I got pregnant, it was no surprise I was having a girl. I mean, duh… I had wanted it, right? Just as I had "known" I'd have my mini-me. My pregnancy was uneventful, and as far as I knew and was told, it was normal.

I had never been pregnant before, so I didn't know she wasn't moving enough—in fact, not even close to the right amount. At my weekly stress tests near the end of my pregnancy, the nurse had to zap her over and over again to get her to move. I even drank juice at breakfast and had a Pepsi on my way to those appointments, and she still wouldn't move. But since nothing showed up on any tests during my prenatal appointments, "it wasn't a concern," they said.

All seemed to be going okay. But as her delivery date approached, all of a sudden, I didn't want to give birth. I felt almost a sense of dread. I started to think, maybe I really didn't want kids and this was a terrible mistake. My excitement was gone. I'd never felt like that before.

I thought it was nerves. Sure, I was scared to deliver. Who isn't, their first time? But looking back now, it was deeper than that. It was almost as if I didn't want the peace to end of her being safe in my belly. Or, to be honest, the peace of my life as I knew it.

I used to go into Ava's room and look at her empty crib, trying to visualize what she would look like lying there. Or rock in the rocking chair, trying to picture feeding her, but I just couldn't see it. I couldn't visualize the baby I'd dreamed of since I was a little girl. I could not picture her at all, no matter how hard I tried. The baby I was about to give birth to! What was happening? This had *never* happened before.

I shrugged it off as the nerves, but now I can see what was happening. My intuition knew something was off, and my heart knew something was off. My brain just hadn't gotten the memo yet. I truly had no idea just how my life was going to change once Ava left the comfort of my womb. But I was about to find out.

That little mini-me I had dreamed of my entire life was not the baby girl I gave birth to. From the moment my Ava entered the world, the Lisa who'd brought me up to that moment was gone, forever changed...

In the chapters ahead, I'll take you along with me through some of the hardest seasons of my life—the medical crises, the grief, the isolation, the losing of myself. And also, how I am finding my way back. Not quickly. Not cleanly. But slowly, and in pieces.

My story doesn't unfold in neat chronological order. Healing rarely does. These chapters are told as they were lived—overlapping, intertwining, sometimes revisiting the same moments from different angles. Together, they form the story that shaped me.

My hope is that, in my story, you will recognize your own strength—even if you can't see it yet.

Unexpected Arrival

I thought Ava's birth would feel magical.
Instead, it felt impersonal, like she wasn't mine at all.
Maybe my heart knew something my mind
wasn't prepared to see.

June 9, 2003. It was a rainy summer day, with cooler than usual temperatures for June in New Hampshire. Was in the sixties and dreary on that morning when my husband, Manny and I headed to the hospital for my planned induction. I wasn't having any complications that warranted an induction, and I've completely forgotten why the doctor scheduled it, since there was no medical urgency or stated reason. Back in those days, I just did whatever the doctors told me. I mean, they are the experts, right?

When we checked in, they got us into our room right away. I remember walking around, thinking, *Holy shit… I am not leaving this room until Ava is born.*

For some strange reason, it just didn't feel real anymore. I started to feel detached from what was happening, like I was acting out a role or something. It wasn't rooted in fear, because I wasn't afraid. I just felt like I was somewhere I wasn't supposed to be, but at the same time I knew I was. Sort of like déjà vu, but I hadn't been through anything like this before.

I got all "moved in" and comfy cozy in my bed. They started me on Pitocin around 8:00, and not much happened for a long time. They ended up breaking my water at some point, to move things along. And we still waited. I think I felt my first contraction later in the afternoon, around 4:00.

I don't remember too many details of the day, except for feeling super-pumped I still was able to see *Live with Regis and Kelly* that day (my favorite show to watch with my mom, when I was on early maternity leave). I remember a killer lunch and also one memory I would love to forget—the epidural from Hell.

My body did not like the epidural at all. My body started shaking all over non-stop from the moment they gave it to me until Ava was born seven hours later. I trembled violently from head to toe. It doesn't seem like much, but at the time it was absolute torture. I felt so uncomfortable. The shaking continued for hours and became so intense, it started to hurt... I couldn't move at all and was shaking so much, I kept bouncing down the bed.

Not being able to move myself meant I had to keep asking people to boost me up every fifteen minutes. Being so shy and not wanting to be a pain in the ass, I felt so bad. Asking them to stop the epidural was never even a thought, because again, I'm not the expert.

After Ava made her debut at 11:00 p.m. that night, the delivery nurse put her on my chest and congratulated us on our new baby girl. This was the moment I had been waiting for, dreaming about, and envisioning forever. I had played that magical moment over and over in my mind since I was a little girl.

I was expecting overwhelming feelings of love for her and such joy of becoming a mother. I'd envisioned myself crying because of the intense love and the bond I had longed for, that a mother and her newborn share, which I had seen my friends and family experience. It was finally my turn to see what that felt like!

But there was no bond. There was no emotional experience. There were no tears of joy; there were no tears at all. No magical moment. Nothing. The baby who had been a part of me for nine months didn't even feel like mine. It was like she was a stranger.

I felt so awkward, having her on my chest, and I couldn't wait until they took her off. Not only did I not have any "bond," it was almost as if I didn't want her around me at all, right after she was born.

This actually frightened me, because I am quite a love bug. I had a deep desire to be a mother my entire life. I'd played out the scenario when I'd meet my baby for the first time in my mind over and over again. How beautiful it would be. How absolutely magical it would be, that Manny and I had created this human, a true gift from God. A miracle would be placed in my hands. How could I *not* feel any emotion about that?

Another thing that frightened me was that I am known to cry over anything remotely touching. TV commercials, greeting cards, elderly couples holding hands, etc. Don't even think about taking me to a Disney movie in public—it's embarrassing. Yet here I was, with my brand-new baby whom I had dreamed of since I was a little girl, and she felt foreign to me. Not only that, but my eyes were as dry as the Sahara Desert. Not even a hint of a tear.

I didn't say anything to anyone, because how could I? I decided to keep it to myself and hoped it would work itself out. I can now say, twenty-two years later, the bond my daughter and I have today is like no other, but I can also say that my reaction to her birth was because I now know My People sensed something was up. (I'll explain who "My People" are and what they represent later in the book; they become a major part of navigating my journey with Ava.)

As far as I knew, when Ava was born, she had no issues. I didn't ask what her APGAR scores were, as I honestly didn't care. All I was truly concerned with was if she had ten fingers and ten toes and did not have Down syndrome. I was so worried about her having Down syndrome and having a challenging life, trying to be accepted, or being made fun of. I used to think, if she'd had Trisomy 21, her life would be awful. Looking back, I can't help but think maybe my fear was not that *her* life would be awful, but *my* life would be awful. Because, if you've ever met anyone with Down syndrome, you know that is the furthest thing from the truth! So naive I was…

After delivering Ava, they moved me, Manny, and Ava into our private room. After a pretty tiring day and after smashing an insane amount of food, I finally was able to shut down and get some well-deserved rest. That didn't last long, though, because a nurse came into our room in the middle of the night to take Ava to the NICU. She said our daughter was not regulating her body temperature and her blood sugars were low. They told us not to worry, to get some sleep, and that we could go see her in the NICU at 9:00 a.m.

I did what I was told and didn't really worry too much, because they'd told me it was pretty common, and she'd be fine. They said that lots of babies have these issues, and, well, I just accepted that because, again, *they are the experts*. They see newborns all the time, and at this point, I was just a first-time mom who hadn't even bonded with her baby yet. So, who was I to question anything? I just did what they told me and took every word they said as fact.

Ava also had a poor suck and took forever to finish each feed. They once again said it was not uncommon. She was a little-bitty, weighing just 6.1 pounds. They said she'd gain her strength and be chugging the bottles in no time. So, when she lost weight and they again told me not to worry, I didn't. Even when we saw no improvement, I just kept telling myself it would all just click for Ava, and this would be a memory.

While in the NICU, I acted like everything was okay, but inside, I was a mess. The fact that my daughter felt foreign to me was still my little secret. But I had just had a baby, so I started to play the "woe is me" card to get out of feeding her or changing her. I was "tired" and often asked Manny to do feeds and diapers or just to let the nurses do it. In all honesty, I just didn't feel comfortable doing those things.

Manny seemed to just ease into his new role. I was kind of jealous of him, because he was head-over-heels in love with Ava from the first moment he laid eyes on her. I'd use silly excuses like I was hurting from the delivery or had to go smoke a cigarette or three, so I didn't have to go back right away to care for her or play my role as a mom. That was exactly what it felt like to me–playing a role. Nothing felt real.

We stayed in the hospital for four days, and when we went home, I kept up the "woe is me" mentality. To be fair, I had reason to be upset about the lack of bonding with Ava and then adding in the four-day NICU stay was a lot to process. I was trying to wrap my head around my emotions, while also trying to deal with it all alone. Being thrown into a stressful situation all at the same time was *a lot*.

On top of that, I was hurt that Manny wasn't taking care of *me*! Being pregnant, while I loved it, is a lot on your body. Delivery is pretty major for any woman to go through, so I think any new mom expects a little special treatment after that.

Manny had always been very thoughtful and made me feel like I was the most important thing in the world, back when we were dating. He stopped doing that kind of stuff after we got married, but this was different. I'd just given birth to his first child! So, I honestly was looking forward to what he would do to make me feel special after having Ava. I dreamed of a little extra pampering from him, a little something special to make me feel appreciated.

But, just like the delivery, it was not what I had envisioned. There was no pampering, no special treatment. No anything. Was I acting like a diva? Maybe, but it's not every day that you push a human out of your body.

Unlike Manny, I'd planned ahead. In my hospital bag, I had packed a gift I'd bought for Manny months before. I was so excited to give it to him: it was a new baseball hat that said Best Dad and a card. My excitement was too much, so I actually had him get it out of my bag in the delivery room, before Ava was even born. I had been waiting so long to give it to him and felt super-proud of myself for taking the time to help make him feel special, when it's usually just about the mothers.

So, that is why I couldn't wait to see what he got for me! I had lots of friends who were already moms, and their husbands spoiled them after the baby was born. It wasn't just about a push present—they were just so good at taking care of their wives, now mother to their child, in general. Like I said, carrying and birthing a baby is a lot of work! And now, it was finally my turn. Or so I thought.

When Manny didn't give me anything in the hospital, I just thought he might have forgotten to pack it. When we got home, I remember asking him if he forgot to pack my gift. I was kind of joking, because I really didn't think he wasn't going to do anything special for me or that he'd forgotten. He used to be *so* romantic, so I just knew he'd take care of me.

His response? He said he didn't forget to pack it because he didn't get me anything. Nothing. Not even a card or a gold star sticker for a job well done. What in the actual you-know-what was happening? I felt so hurt, so left out, so unseen. He'll tell you today that he doesn't get into that stuff. While he didn't mean to hurt me, it felt like a punch in the stomach.

I truly believed I had gotten the shit end of the deal. I gave up my body for nine months, was in labor for seventeen hours, slept at the hospital for four days, and now had to care for this baby all day, while he just went back to work. No extra nothing. Thinking back to that time now, I can't help but believe I was acting like a spoiled little bitch. Maybe it was hormones. Maybe it was again My People, who knew that things would never be the same. It was as if they knew I needed to be taken care of because, at that moment, I was going to need that extra support to navigate the unknown life ahead.

After we got home, Ava continued to have issues with her feeds. It took forever to give her each bottle. Luckily, my mom lived in an in-law apartment attached to my home, so she could do some of the feeds while Manny was at work.

She would come over and watch Ava to let me nap during the day or let me escape the house to make Dunkin's runs. She even made most of our meals and did all of our laundry. And let me tell you, I took full advantage of all of that. Finally, someone was taking care of *me*. Little did I know, the feeling sorry for myself, spoiled-brat mentality was about to change in a major way just a few short months later.

Feeding wasn't the only thing that was a struggle with Ava. She slept *a lot*. Being a first-time mom, I had no idea that babies aren't supposed to sleep all day. Ava would have slept 24/7, if I let her. Manny and I had to set our alarm clock to wake up every few hours and feed her at night, or she'd sleep right through. She also never cried for food or cried at all, for that matter, so I'd have to wake her up for each bottle, spend what seemed like forever giving it to her, and then she'd sleep again until her next feed. Wash, rinse, repeat. I thought she was just a good baby. That was, until her four-month checkup.

Her pediatrician was my age, still new at her career, but I instantly fell in love with her. She was extremely sweet, and there was just something about her that immediately felt right. So, when she seemed concerned that Ava wasn't holding her head up yet, I got concerned, too. Ava had a pretty big head, which could have been the reason she wasn't holding it up yet, but my pediatrician still wanted us to head to Children's Hospital in Boston for an ultrasound, to rule out any issues, specifically hydrocephalus.

Children's Hospital? In Boston? *What*? Isn't Children's Hospital where those kids go who are on TV? The really sick kids? The ones with wires and tubes who need special care? My baby was fine, I told her. I mentioned, in case she didn't notice, Ava's dad has a pretty big noggin. But even with that, the pediatrician still wanted to rule it out. *Sigh.*

That was when I first turned to the Internet for what would be twenty-two-plus years of never-ending research for Ava. I educated myself on hydrocephalus and found that it is treated with a shunt surgically placed in the head of the child. OMG.

That "woe is me" mentality? Feeling sorry for myself for not getting pampered? Gone.

That bond that I didn't feel? Not even a thought any longer.

From that moment, the pain I felt, the fear I felt, the dread I felt, it was all as if it was *me* who was having the ultrasound. Like it was *my* life that would be affected by a potentially bad outcome. The dreams of Ava running and playing with friends at recess were now replaced with fear of being made fun of for having a shunt or complications from surgery or worse. With surgeries, doctor appointments, special care. Our carefree life could possibly be replaced with a life of worry and complications.

It hit me pretty hard. I didn't have any friends or family whose kids had any issues, so this could potentially be something I'd have to do alone. If no one had experienced anything like this, how could they understand my feelings, never mind help support me? That scared me to death.

Also, I questioned how could I be the right person to deal with this for Ava? I had struggled just feeling like her mother, so how could I be trusted to keep her safe? Was this something that I'd caused in my pregnancy? Was this my fault? Was she paying for choices I had made? My mind was in a constant state of panic, regret, fear, and also dread.

But then the weirdest thing happened. One day, while I was lost in those thoughts, my mindset suddenly just... shifted. Like a switch went off. The thought popped into my head that, whatever is going to happen is going to happen, no matter how I feel about it. It doesn't matter if I stay up worrying nightly or sleep contently like a baby. Whatever was destined to happen was going to happen.

Why am I thinking about all of the "what ifs? Why am I letting go of the moment I am living right now? I mean, there are so many things that may never happen, so why am I using my energy stressing over something that may never come into existence?

Shortly after that realization, I shared a private moment with my mom that I will never forget. I was sitting on my couch with Ava lying on my chest after a feed. My mom walked into the living room as I was just sitting there in silence, rubbing Ava's back. I smiled at her when I saw her walk in.

She said to me, "Wow, you are so calm, even though you are going through so much. I am extremely proud of you."

Those words were very powerful to me. She made me feel seen, feel important, and most of all, feel capable of handling whatever was to come. That ended up being one of the most important moments of my life, and her words would help get me through some very challenging times in the years to come.

Turns out, I actually didn't have to worry, because Ava ended up not having hydrocephalus. Her not being able to lift her head was due to her oversized pumpkin and a thing called *hypotonia*. Low muscle tone.

Manny and I were like, this is a joke, right? *Low muscle tone?* I mean, we met at the gym, he competed in body building, and working out was a huge part of our life. How could *our* kid have low muscle tone? There was no way. It was actually kind of funny.

Because of that, we both didn't worry a whole lot about the hypotonia. I thought, just watch, she'll turn out to be one of those kids who just gets up and walks out of the blue. Like a super-kid. I thought she'd snap out of it.

I maintained that mentality over the next eleven months and kept waiting for Ava to snap out of it all through the physical therapy appointments, feeding therapy appointments, and occupational therapy appointments, even though she wasn't making any progress. I believed, *It will happen. She just needs more time. She will show them just how strong she really is.* After all, she was my kid, and if she had half the determination I have, she'd blow right past her milestones.

I continued to work with her daily on strengthening her trunk to be able to sit, playing sign language videos for her, and trying to teach her how to sign, trying different bottles/nipples/sippy cups to find one that she would "like" or would help her to drink more easily. My entire day was dedicated to helping her break through this barrier that she was destined to overcome. I just knew, if I kept working with her, kept believing in her, and kept faith in her, I would get to share the great news: *SHE DID IT!*

That was until May 28, 2004, when everything changed.
She had her first grand mal seizure.

14 Minutes

I wasn't ready.
I wasn't brave.
But in 14 minutes, I became both.

Everyone has something they are afraid of. It can be full-blown phobias that control how you live each day or just overwhelming fears that you avoid experiencing at all costs. For me, here are four things that I am afraid of.

First, I have a pretty severe fear of people throwing up, and I have come to find out this is a very common phobia. It actually has a name: *emetophobia.*

My second fear is spiders, followed by seizures, and lastly, emergency rooms. Other than spiders and the occasional stomach bug, my phobias really aren't things I typically need to worry about or even deal with too often, if ever. So, for the most part, these fears didn't really affect the way I lived my life at all.

The worst and strongest fear I have is emetophobia. It is so bad, if someone even says their stomach hurts, my heart starts racing, I get weak in the knees, and I start getting shaky, and I get the hell away from them in a hurry. After that, I continue to freak out for the rest of the day… Are they sick? Will I catch it? Did they throw up? If I see someone throw up, I keep replaying that image in my brain over and over. Not just for the next hour or so, no. More like for months. Just seeing it in my mind keeps the mental cycle going for days... Hearing it? Nope. Cannot do it. Even when I throw up, I have to put the shower on, faucet on, and bathroom fan on before I can "safely" throw up. *Ugh.*

My arachnophobia. Don't need to explain that one. The bigger, hairier, and juicier the spider, the bigger my fear. I am typically a lover of all creatures and feel that everything has its purpose in life, but spiders, they are different. I have no love for them. None.

If they come into *my* house, then they need to die. Like empty a can of Raid, smash it until you can't tell what it was, and even with that, flush the guts down the toilet, so they can't pull a Terminator character and merge back together to come and get me.

Well, if I'm being honest, someone *else* has to do the killing, smashing, and disposal of the body, because I'm too scared that I might miss, and then it'll touch me. Plus, I just can't "feel" the squishing. Maybe it makes them turn more into a living creature than a nightmare with eight legs. Maybe I don't want to carry the responsibility of the killing on my conscience. Who knows? Either way—*gross.*

If they are outside? That is their house. I just try to calmly walk away and let them do their spider things. Like, my bad for entering your territory. I'll quietly leave and let you live your scary life, just not near me.

The fear of emergency rooms kind of goes hand in hand with emetophobia, since throwing up is happening all over the ER. But even without the throwing up part, something about walking into the ER just makes me freak out. I can't even sit in the waiting room. I have to always be standing near the door. I feel safe near the door, like I can easily escape. Safe so I don't have to hear all the sounds people make or possibly see someone throw up, collapse, or worse. Plus, at the exit, I am farther away from the cooties.

And lastly, seizures. Kind of crazy, because I had seizures as a baby. I was one of the lucky ones who had a reaction to the measles vaccine back in the early seventies. Lucky for my mom, even though I had a handful of grand mal seizures in one day, it wasn't a lifelong issue.

Most people go about living their lives never knowing they have a fear of seizures. That was definitely the case for me. I didn't find out I had that fear until I witnessed my first seizure, and that was it for me. Another new fear unlocked.

I was introduced to seizures when I was about twenty years old. I had a boyfriend who coached our local Pop Warner football team. To be supportive of his coaching, I went to some of the games. At one game, I was sitting in the bleachers when, all of a sudden, the whole bench I was sitting on started to shake. I was like, *what the heck*? It felt like an earthquake or something. Or like someone was stomping their feet vigorously or shaking the stands.

When I turned to look, I couldn't believe what I was seeing. The woman sitting right next to me—like cheek to cheek on the bleacher—was having a full-blown grand mal seizure: arms flailing, legs jerking, her whole body shaking, foaming at the mouth, and all. Holy freaking shitballs!

I hightailed my ass off of those bleachers so fast and ran to the other side of the field in absolute and total freakout mode. I probably looked like one of those cartoons that leaves the trail of dust behind them, I went so fast! Forrest Gump would have been proud of me.

What the hell was that? I had never seen a seizure in my life. Sure, I'd heard of them. Heck, I even had them myself as a baby (measles vaccine). But seen them? Nope. Man, that was scary! After experiencing that, I never wanted to see that again. Like ever. Because of that event, I didn't go to any more of the football games that year or ever. I also made sure that anything her kids would be at, I would stay far away. I never wanted to see her and risk seeing another seizure ever again. That was some scary shit.

After that event, I was lucky enough to not encounter another seizure. I didn't even think about seizures anymore and felt like, well, I can check that off my list. What were the chances I'd have to experience that again? Slim to none. Now, I could go live the rest of my life without witnessing such a traumatic event. Thank God.

My smooth-sailing, seizure-free life lasted fourteen years, until a beautiful, sunny, warm spring day in May 2004.

Ava was eleven months old, but still a total noodle. She still couldn't sit up on her own due to her hypotonia, so I spent a lot of my day helping her work on building up the strength to do it. For Ava, it was just us playing together all day, but I was sneaky with my workouts for her.

Since it was a gorgeous spring day, I thought I'd take her outside to do one of her "workouts" in the fresh air, near my dad, while he did some yardwork. Maybe she'd be encouraged to work harder and show off for her Bimpy. She adored him, so if she was going to perform for anyone, he was definitely high on her list.

I still remember how good it felt to be out in the sunshine, the warmth on my skin, and feeling super-proud of Ava for how hard she was working. I even got her to hold a tripod sitting position for about fifteen seconds! That was quite an accomplishment for her. It was a good day.

Not just a good day… the first day I felt truly content since I'd had her. Finally, she had made some noticeable progress in her strength. I remember feeling so much hope for her, and I almost felt like a "regular" mom.

"So, this is what it feels like when your child does new things on their own," I thought. Really awesome! Just as I had planned, she was going to snap out of this. I felt a sense of freedom I hadn't felt yet with Ava. Kind of like the relief you experience when you've been wearing tight pants all day then finally get to the comfort of your own home and unzip those pants… Yeah, kind of like that.

Unfortunately, that feel-good feeling didn't last long.

Later that day, just a few short hours later, I had Ava sitting in her highchair at the table while I cleaned up her bottle from lunch. Even though she wasn't having meals yet due to her feeding issues, I wanted her to start getting used to sitting in her chair for her three meals a day. I wanted to mimic mealtimes, so she could ease into eating solid food a bit more easily with an already set schedule. I gave her the bottle at typical mealtimes while in the chair, all while working with her and encouraging her to drink more efficiently and maybe, eventually, hold her own bottle.

My back was to her for a few minutes while I was at the sink. Even though I wasn't there for long, I peeked at her often to be sure she was still doing okay and hadn't flopped over in her seat or tipped to the side due to her weak trunk strength, the hypotonia. Even though I had her positioned well and buckled in, that noodle in her always seemed to want to flop over. She could be totally fine one minute, and the next, smash her face from falling forward or be close to falling over the edge.

Sometimes, I would wash the bottles standing sideways at the sink, but this particular day, since I felt that freedom and had a sense of hope that things were progressing, I didn't stand sideways. I kept my back to her. You know, like the "regular" moms do.

The last time I turned around, she wasn't sitting up straight, but I had no idea what she was doing. She had slumped over, facing down, and she was shaking all over. I thought, *Is she having a laughing fit? Is she stuck? Is she hurt? Is she crying?* She didn't really cry, so that couldn't be it. *What the heck is she doing?*

She was kind of bouncing like she was having a laughing fit, but was she? I wasn't so sure. All of those thoughts happened in seconds while my body went toward her going full speed, just those few steps.

I lifted her head up and, since I'd never seen her do this before, I was hoping to see her big, cheeky grin smiling at me in a laughing fit. That was absolutely not was I saw. I just stared at her in disbelief. She wasn't laughing or even smiling at all, but what *was* she doing?

Somehow, I knew I had to get her out of that chair immediately. Instinct took over, and I unlocked the safety straps. When I picked her up and could feel the rhythmic shaking in my hands, I was instantly brought back to that day fourteen years ago on the bleachers at the Pop Warner football game…

NO! Holy shit, she is having a seizure! *No*! *No*! *NO*! Not again, not *my* baby! What do I do?

I couldn't run away this time. I had to stay. I had to help her. I was immediately filled with an intense feeling of both dread and fear.

I sprinted to the door that separates my parents' in-law apartment from my house, and I kicked it over and over as hard as I could while trying to hold her in my arms as she continued to seize.

At the top of my lungs, I screamed for my mother, *"HELP! HELP ME! I NEED YOU!"*

She came running through the door and immediately knew what was going on when she saw us. She told me to put Ava down in the hallway near the door while she called 911.

I don't remember anything from the time I put her on the floor until the time the EMTs arrived, but my mom sure did. She told me, while she was on the phone with the 911 dispatcher, I was hovering over Ava, cradling her head in my hands so it wouldn't bang off the floor. I rocked my body back and forth and kept saying, "Please don't die. Please don't die. Please don't leave me."

I can't imagine how much my mother's heart must have broken that day. Having to watch her granddaughter seizing her brains out and also watch the life her own daughter "should have had" end from that moment forward. It probably also brought back some not-so-great memories from when I had the seizures at about the same age as Ava was. I sure wish she was alive today, so I could thank her for her strength in that moment.

Fourteen minutes later, the EMTs arrived. Yes, *fourteen* long and horrific minutes while I watched her seizing. It could have been another minute or two before I saw her at the beginning of the seizure, since my back was turned, and I don't know how long it lasted in the ambulance before they gave her the rescue meds to get the seizure to stop. But even with that, fourteen minutes of having a grand mal seizure cannot be good. You don't need to be an expert to know that.

My worries: *Will she have brain damage? Why did this happen? Did I do something to cause this? Was it something in the grass where I had her sitting? Did I push her too hard? Is she going to die?*

As I waited helplessly outside the ambulance, my mind was going in circles until they told me I could get in to see her. My body was in fight-or-flight mode for the first time, and unfortunately, as I found out that day, when Ava has a seizure, it triggers my bowels. My eyes see a seizure and somehow my bowels say, "It's go time!" What I think was happening was my body had switched into protective mama mode, stayed strong, and did what it needed to do during the seizure, but when the dust settled, it realized it had just been face-to-face with one of its phobias.

I know it's crazy to share my nervous poops, but trust me, it ends up being significant later on in my journey.

Once I was out of the bathroom and they had finally stabilized Ava, I hopped inside the ambulance, and we headed to the ER. The EMT asked me if what she was wearing was something important or something I didn't want to get ruined.

I was confused, because what did her clothes have to do with a seizure? I said no, and then he tore her onesie in half all the way down to get access to her body. *Oh my God.*

I can still hear the tearing of that onesie clear as day, decades later. I saved that onesie, along with her first oxygen mask from her first sedation, her first pair of AFO braces, and her bag full of hospital bracelets from various inpatient stays, tests, surgeries, etc., because I had hoped to go through all of these "trinkets" with her someday when she was grown up and had "snapped out of it." We could reminisce and be equally proud and grateful of how far she had come since then. Even though that day will unfortunately never come for us, I just can't seem to get rid of that onesie. It has such a hold on me. Looking back now, it was as if, when the EMT ripped the onesie, he also ripped my chance of a "normal" life at the same time.

When we got to the hospital, they evaluated Ava in the ER, and they didn't find anything wrong. Nothing that would have caused the seizure. No fever, no infection, nothing. Labs were perfect. So, to keep an eye on her, they admitted us to stay overnight.

Manny spent the night with me and Ava. The plan was we would take turns sleeping while one of us stayed awake to watch Ava for any more seizures.

That night was a turning point for me. That first overnight stay was the first time I realized that I am incapable of sleeping or being away from Ava when she is not at her baseline.

I physically could not sleep, couldn't leave to use the bathroom, nothing. I had to watch her and know firsthand she was okay. That night, I also realized not only did I have that special bond between a mother and her child, but it was stronger than I could ever have imagined.

Ava didn't seize again that night. *Thank God,* I thought. They discharged us and told us to come back if she had another seizure. They gave us a referral to a neurologist to follow up with and sent us on our way. That was it. They were done with us.

That was great news, except I didn't want to go home. I didn't want to leave. I didn't want to let go of the safety of the hospital, the nurses, the doctors. The machines that could see things I couldn't. The medicines that could do magic and stop her seizures when I couldn't. I wasn't ready. I was scared to death.

I didn't want to have to do this without the hospital staff. I didn't sign up for this. I didn't ask for this. I didn't *want* this. I felt such an enormous sense of helplessness. It felt like I was being forced to start living a nightmare. Not the best feeling to have when thinking about taking care of your own child. Not at all.

I was so freaking jealous of Manny because he was able to go to work. He had no choice but to leave the house and focus on something else for the majority of his day. He had to work, because he was the only income. But by him going to work, he wouldn't have to watch her every waking hour, waiting for and anticipating *another* seizure. He wouldn't have to fear going to the bathroom, washing out bottles, or getting the mail. He wouldn't need someone to come and watch Ava while he showered. I couldn't do anything without coverage, and I could never let her out of my sight.

I also started to become jealous of every mom who didn't have to deal with this. I envied them not knowing what it looks like to see their only child, their tiny baby girl, thrash and turn blue while waiting for the EMTs. To feel like their baby was going to die and all they could do was watch it happen helplessly. To not have to live in fear every moment of their life, waiting for it to happen again. When we got discharged, every person I saw on the way out of the hospital had me wondering if they'd had to deal with seizures and how lucky they were if they didn't. I was leaving the hospital to begin a whole new life. A life I had never imagined would be mine to live. And I didn't want it.

I had already been jealous of moms who had babies that could feed easily, could sit on their own, crawl and babble, make funny sounds and raspberries, and play with their toys, while mine didn't do any of that. Now, not only did I not have a baby who could do those things, I had a baby who had had a seizure. It made all of the other things Ava was struggling with seem so simple. I was mad at myself for complaining about her issues before this, because I didn't realize just how lucky I had been until Ava had that first seizure. Yes, you read that right. *First seizure*. It was just the beginning for Ava.

After the overnight stay, we had the follow-up appointment with a local neurologist the next week. The neurologist we wanted worked at a hospital an hour and a half away and had a two-year waitlist. We went on the waitlist and planned to see the local specialist until we could get in to see the one we wanted. From what I had heard, he was 100% worth the wait.

I remember having an off feeling about the local neurologist, but I let it slide. Kind of like that "knowing" I'd had before, but this felt a little different. I just thought it was me not wanting to see her because of the situation, not because she wasn't a "good" doctor. Lately, I hadn't been trusting my gut feelings, since I had been incredibly wrong about everything with Ava so far.

I would learn later that those gut feelings were very much still there, I just hadn't yet built up my confidence in being Ava's mother to notice them. Those gut feelings from my pre-Ava life transformed into My People, and they would never steer me wrong.

After the visit with the local neurologist, she ordered an MRI, an EEG, and put Ava on a daily preventative seizure medication. She also prescribed a rescue med for Ava just in case: Diastat. Rescue meds are to be given when someone has a seizure that just won't stop, or if they last more than a few minutes. I didn't think we would ever need it, but I took it anyway. In the ER, I had been told by the pediatrician and the neurologist that sometimes this just happens. Sometimes kids have one seizure and that's it. One and done.

So, once again, I thought Ava would be that kid—the one who overcomes it all and just snaps out of it. My thought was reinforced when the neurologist told me that Ava's EEG and MRI were both normal. Of course they were! She was going to be just fine. This would all be a memory that we'd look back on someday. Ava was definitely going to be okay. Maybe my instinct was going to be spot on after all!

After a few months passed, I started to relax a little bit, starting to exhale and feel more confident that it was a fluke thing and I'd never have to experience seeing her seize again. Starting to get that "normal mom" feeling again. Then… *BAM.* She had another grand mal. And it was another doozy.

I am so thankful that it was July 2, the first day of the long weekend, and Manny was home. He was actually holding her when the seizure started. The instructions they'd given us if it happened again was to administer the rescue medicine if her seizure hadn't stopped after four minutes had passed.

I ripped Ava out of Manny's hands so I could take over. I needed to feel everything, watch her closely, and be sure she was breathing. It wasn't that I didn't trust him. I just felt like I *had* to be in control; I had to notice every little detail to tell the doctor. I had to be the one who held her and helped to keep her safe. I instantly became the voice she didn't have. I have no idea where those thoughts came from, but man oh man, over the years, those kinds of thoughts have saved her life.

Holding Ava for those four minutes felt like four years. Watching your child have a grand mal seizure, gasping for breath, thrashing violently in your arms, losing her color, while waiting for four minutes. Tick… Tock… Tick… Tock… It was torture. Then it dawned on me: Manny had never seen a seizure when he said, "Is this what her first seizure looked like?"

Well, shit. Poor Manny. Seeing her little body go through a seizure is a lot to take in, and now I felt so badly for how I was jealous of him. I remember thinking how Ava was his daughter, too, and how selfish I had been for being jealous of him for leaving each day. What if he felt like he had to be close to her like I did? What if it was eating him up to leave us each day but, being a man, kept his feelings bottled up inside? In that moment, I felt like not only was I trying to keep Ava alive, I was also making sure Manny was doing okay with it. Man, were we going through a lot in that moment as a couple, as a family.

At the four-minute mark, we gave her the rescue med, the Diastat, and thank God we'd already called the ambulance, because she instantly turned blue. Not bluish, *BLUE*. She did stop seizing immediately, and when she turned blue, we thought she'd also stopped breathing. Her body looked completely lifeless. We thought she was dead.

Luckily, right at that moment, the ambulance arrived. Once again, they whisked her into the back of the ambulance, and just like last time, off I ran to the bathroom…

This time, when we got to the ER, they didn't want to keep her there in their hospital. They said that another hospital in the state had a children's hospital with many more pediatric specialists and testing made for children. This other hospital is an hour and a half away, but it also just so happened to have the neurologist we were on the waitlist for.

I was kind of upset, because it felt like they didn't want to treat her. Didn't want to deal with her. But I am so glad she went, because with that transfer, I realized this other hospital, because they specialized in pediatric care, had testing that catered more to pediatrics. It would be safer and better for her all around, if she was transferred. Not a one-size-fits-all like the hospital we were at. So, off we went. I rode in the back of the ambulance with Ava, and Manny followed behind in our minivan for the hour-and-a-half ride.

What a way to start the long Fourth of July holiday weekend. While I was so grateful that Manny wouldn't miss work and could be with me without worry, I felt bad that the EMTs had to spend their July 2 driving a total of three hours to and fro, transporting Ava. I'm sure they had better things to do.

I ended up sharing my thoughts with the amazing EMT who was in the back with us, and she was so sweet about it. She assured me they would much rather be transporting my beautiful baby than dealing with people blowing their fingers off with fireworks. She was right and was exactly what I needed in that moment. She calmed me, talking about her amazing patriotic nails she'd gotten done for the holiday and just chit-chatting with me like we were at a coffee shop. She made the ride somewhat bearable, and I will never forget her.

When we arrived at the ER at the hospital up north, once again, after checking Ava out, they couldn't find anything wrong. No virus, no fever, no UTI, and all labs looked good. And just like the other hospital, this one also wanted to keep her overnight for observation. Ava was stable, but there were still no answers as to why she was having seizures.

Once again, I kept an eye on her all night, scared to freaking death that another one was going to happen. It didn't. We were discharged the next morning and told to come back if she seized again. Ava seemed healthy, with no signs of infection or illness, so there wasn't much more they could do for her. We went home that next morning, on July 3.

On July 4, we were back at the hospital.

Another grand mal. Another bathroom run. Another transfer from the ER in an ambulance to the hospital up north. But this time was different. That neurologist we were on the waitlist for, two years out? It turned out he was at the hospital that day, on the pediatrics unit, checking on some patients of his that were inpatient. Though we hadn't had the official appointment yet in his office, we were considered a patient of his, so he stopped by Ava's room. I cannot tell you how absolutely pumped we were to get to meet this man and have him lay eyes on our Ava.

This man, this neurologist, was very well known and respected by so many in the field and is truly the best of the best. He had been on Oprah back in the nineties for diagnosing two siblings after years and years of no answers. With that diagnosis, he got them from being wheelchair-bound to being able to run around and play with their peers! I'm sorry, what?

I felt like it was fate that we were seeing him, because I just knew he would figure this out. Like *he* was the missing link to getting her "fixed," and we'd end up being another amazing diagnosis story of his. I couldn't wait! I just knew he was going to help Ava the way he'd helped those siblings, because, again, she was going to snap out of it. I almost wanted to ask him if he was up for another Oprah show—ha-ha!

That summer, Ava did have yet another grand mal, in August, and even though she didn't require the rescue meds, we were instructed once again to head to the hospital up north. We lucked out again, because our future neurologist was on call, so he was the one to care for her during this stay. I say future, because we still hadn't had our official first appointment in the office yet, but he was already getting to know her quite well. Because of that, he decided to switch her seizure medication, which helped to keep the seizures under control for a little bit.

While her grand mal seizures kept quiet for the time being, Ava did end up in the hospital again after having the first of her many status epilepticus episodes. Status epilepticus is when a seizure lasts more than five minutes or when seizures are very close together and the person doesn't recover consciousness between them. At this point, Ava had officially been diagnosed with epilepsy. Her seizures weren't considered a fluke any longer, but no one yet knew why they were happening.

Ava's first status epilepticus was brought on by a new type of seizure she started to have: myoclonic seizures. These seizures look much different than the grand mals.

Myoclonic seizures look sort of like when someone comes up behind you, scares you, and you jump. Her arms and legs would flail up suddenly like she'd been spooked. She would jump, make a little cry, and be done. That was it, the whole seizure.

In Ava's case, her myoclonic seizures almost always came in clusters and lots of times would lead to a grand mal seizure. If the grand mal wasn't "violent" enough or, as we called it, "a big Kahuna," the process would start all over again. Myoclonics on repeat until the next grand mal. Once she finished a cycle, meaning her brain had had a big enough grand mal to make it happy, she'd just go to sleep, and that's how we knew it was over. Her body would finally be still, and she would be at complete rest.

Watching Ava go through that was so incredibly hard to endure as a parent. It would literally rip my heart out to watch her suffer so much. Not only was she physically going through absolute hell, she couldn't even communicate how she was feeling to me. Couldn't tell me she was scared or needed a hug or that she was hurting. She could just try to tell me with her eyes. And I couldn't help it stop.

These episodes would be this: seize, cry, seize, cry for maybe an hour or two hours or three hours, each seizure being a minute apart, and then a grand mal, just to repeat the process all over again. The only time I'd ever heard her really cry was during these seizures. And by cry, I mean little whimpers. Her poor little body was going through so much.

The myoclonic seizures don't follow the same seizure rescue protocol as the grand mals. These are so quick, they cannot be treated by waiting for four minutes like the grand mals. Because of that, it's impossible to put a plan of action in place, because every situation is different.

Typically, when Ava was young and we didn't have a lot of seizure experience under our belts, we'd be in contact with the neurologist after each seizure. That was because they didn't know why she was having them and had no idea what could happen or how her body was going to react. Whenever they were considered to progress to status epilepticus, that always meant an urgent trip to the ER. That's because status epilepticus has some pretty serious possible complications, like: brain damage, respiratory failure, heart problems, and even death.

During Ava's first inpatient hospital stays for status epilepticus, they added another medication to her seizure mix. This was more of a short-acting medication and was absolutely a godsend for her myoclonic seizures. Unless she was having an illness, we didn't really see those myoclonic seizures again. If we did, we could give her a small dose of the medication immediately, and it would stop the cycle in its tracks. For the most part, we didn't see any seizures at all for a few years!

When Ava's seizures began in the spring of 2004, I started praying to God nightly. I was raised a Catholic and received all of the sacraments but was never a "practicing" Catholic. Before this, I had never prayed on my own. But now, I would drop to my knees every night before bed and beg God to take the seizures away. Of all of her issues—the feeding difficulties, lack of sitting, crawling, and babbling, and basically any typical baby milestones—the seizures were what I wanted taken away, what I *needed* taken away, in order for her to have a comfortable life. For me to have a comfortable life.

I prayed for a diagnosis that was treatable and would put an end to her seizures. I prayed for a diagnosis that maybe would show she had a lack of a certain vitamin or something that could easily be treated with supplements. And just like I had dreamed all along—she would snap out of it.

I promised God, if my prayers came true, I would forever be in debt to Him for this and would make it my life's mission to help other moms like myself get a diagnosis for their child. I wanted to spread awareness so their children could be diagnosed sooner and not have to go through what Ava had gone through. So that their families would not have to go through what ours had gone through. I dreamed of talking at schools, at churches, at moms' groups, and at hospitals.

Because of my history, how in the past, when I really wanted something badly enough, I got it, I just *knew* God would come through for me. I mean, even though I didn't go to church, I was a good person. I have this insane thing where I can't lie, and I had done all the things right—did well in school, respected my parents, lived at home until I was married, bought a house, and then, a few years later, had Ava. I figured, since I was doing all the things a good Catholic should do (or so I was told), why wouldn't He answer my prayers?

Plus, Ava was truly the sweetest little girl I had ever known. If He really did love His children like I had been taught, then why would He let her continue to suffer? This all felt logical at the time, but boy, was I way off.

During that "honeymoon period" of living seizure-free for those first few years, Ava and I started to come alive! I stopped letting the fear of "what if" she had a seizure in the car or "what if" she had a seizure in the store rule my life. She became my little shopping buddy, and I took her everywhere. We went to all kinds of different stores, plus on Dunkin' Donuts iced-coffee runs, visited Manny at jobs he was doing, and went for walks around the mall. She didn't care where she went; she just loved being out. She was such a happy girl, always smiling, giggling, and for anyone she came in contact with, making everyone's day just a little bit brighter.

At three years old, Ava graduated out of home-based therapies through the state-managed occupational, speech, and physical therapies, so she had to transition to receiving therapies at the local school. She started preschool in their special ed program because of her disabilities, and though I was very scared to have her away from me, she had a blast. She continued in that same school for pre-K and kindergarten.

I am so lucky to have had such an amazing local special ed program, especially at that school. All of the staff were so welcoming to her (and very tolerant to me, always lurking around…), and even though she was the only one in a wheelchair, the only one in diapers, the only one who was tube fed, and the only one who didn't talk, they included her in everything! She began making some progress with hand-over-hand therapies and weight bearing with physical therapy, and she even started to sign "Mama" and "I love you!" I was so very proud of her!

While the fear of seizures never went away, I did become more comfortable with taking her to more and more places farther away from home. Before we went anywhere, though, we always had to map out the nearest emergency room, "just in case." Manny and I even took her to Mystic,

Connecticut for a week to go to the aquarium, Mystic Pizza (duh), and just hang by the pool at the house we rented. It was our first vacation as a family.

Even though things were different for Ava and our family, I was happy with her progress. I still prayed nightly for the seizures to not come back and was keeping up my end of the bargain, researching day and night to help getting her diagnosed. I went on the National Organization for Rare Diseases website every day and read the details about each disease, one by one, to see if she had symptoms. Over the years, I had asked her neurologist to test for many potential diseases I'd found by doing that research, but Ava kept testing negative for all of them. Still, I was determined to find a diagnosis for her and then make it my life's purpose to learn about it and start to spread that awareness. I was on fire for it!

Though we spent many years seizure-free, eventually, that peace did come to an end. Just like before, there was no real trigger or reason for Ava's seizure, which broke the years-long run without any seizures. But this time, the seizure looked different than the others had.

This seizure had her foaming at the mouth, and once it was over, she vomited. Even though I still had my same old bowel reaction, for some reason, this time, I felt like there *was* a reason for these new seizures. They looked totally different from the others, and they were shorter. Plus, they stopped on their own, so she never needed the rescue meds—*thank God*. Because of that, the neurologist sort of agreed and was hoping maybe these were the type of seizure she could eventually grow out of.

He told us that with some forms of epilepsy in children, they can grow out of them by age seven. When he said that, once again, I thought, *this is it!* Maybe she won't snap out of it, but she will *grow* out of it!

The crazy thing about seizures, though, even with so many advancements in medicine, they do whatever the heck they want. There is no rhyme or reason to them. You have no idea when they are coming, and you have no idea if they will ever happen again. You also have no idea if it's going to be a short one or if it's the big one that could end it all. Yes, the one that could end her life. It's one of the many mysteries of the brain.

For someone like me, who needs to know the "why" for everything, this has been the hardest pill for me to swallow. Talk about an adjustment. I've never been the type to just put a Band-Aid on something and call it a day. I always search for the root cause, usually skipping the Band-Aid altogether. Being told that the root cause may never be revealed and also that no one has any idea what my child's future with seizures will be, or her future in general for that matter, that was all equally frustrating and devastating.

But even with that being said, my little hero Ava went into another seizure-free period—this time she hit a whopping four years seizure free!

When Ava had the seizure that broke her four-year seizure-free honeymoon period, she was ten years old. It occurred in the fall, on the day when our whole Laurencio clan got our annual flu vaccinations. We all rolled up our sleeves that day, including my twins who were just over a year old, whom we'd added to the family during this last seizure-free period. (More to come on them later.)

I always made sure all of my kids' vaccines were thimerosal free and never gave them more than one vaccine at a time. Because of that, I wasn't really expecting any type of reaction or injury. It just wasn't on my radar.

Later that night, we were all hanging out on the living room floor, playing together as a family. The twins were acting totally fine, and so was Ava. I was neurotic about checking for spikes in temperatures after any vaccine, even though none of my children ever had a fever, post-vaccination. That didn't stop me from being a serial temperature taker, though.

At one point, I was sitting on the floor. Ava was leaning on me while I propped her up, so she could play with the twins more easily. Like in the past, I thought she had started giggling, because her body began to tremble. But nope. It was another grand mal, and this was another big one.

This one hit particularly hard because now, Manny and I didn't have the "luxury" of caring just for Ava. We also had twins in our care, and they were mobile. My mom wasn't around any longer to step in and help. Saying we were afraid is an understatement. This very situation was one of the main reasons I did *not* want to have more kids. And now, it was happening.

Even though a whole four-and-a-half years had passed since Ava's last grand mal, my bowels definitely remembered what was going on. To my digestive system, it was muscle memory. After Ava's seizure stopped, I had to scoop up the twins and bring them with me to the bathroom, so Manny could keep Ava safe and not have to help them with anything.

We also had a dog running around at the time, and let's just say, the twins were safer with me. It was such a high-stress scenario. Absolute chaos.

I knew without question that this seizure had been triggered by the vaccine Ava had had just hours earlier. But why? She'd had flu vaccines many times before. Why did this one cause her to seize, especially having gone four-and-a-half years seizure-free?

To make matters worse, Ava went on to have a total of ten grand mal seizures over the course of the next few days. She had never had that many massive seizures in a short time her entire life! While I knew with certainty the vaccine did trigger it, I never was able to find out why or what might have happened. Without going into my whole lengthy process of trying to get answers to this reaction, I do want to say, even back then in 2012, when I asked about possible vaccine reactions or when I tried to get specific information about correlations, there were many road blocks. But I know what I saw. I know what happened. But for some reason, that wasn't accepted as fact. So, could that vaccine reaction have made her epilepsy worse? Possibly. Was it a vaccine injury and not just a reaction? Also very possible. Could it have done damage to her already-different brain? Only God knows those answers for certain.

Over the years, seizures still poked their head up from time to time, but usually, it was just one and done. They started acting more like true epilepsy and showed up like a vengeance during a virus or whenever she spiked a fever. It wasn't a number on the thermometer that triggered the seizure; rather, it was the speed at which it got there.

For example, Ava could have a virus with a fever of 104 and not seize. But she could have a minor cold that started out with a fever that spiked suddenly from normal to 102.5 in a short period of time, and that would cause her to seize. Most times, I had no idea she was even coming down with anything until she had a seizure. We always had to take her to the doctor to be checked out and have her urine tested, because she was also lucky enough to have issues with kidney stones and kidney infections in her life.

I will never forget one of those times when she had a seizure out of nowhere. I was getting her meds ready in the kitchen with the baby monitor on, watching her while she snoozed away in the bedroom. Like I've said, I am always watching her. If I am not with her, I always have a camera on her.

I glanced away from the camera for one second, and when I looked back, she was in a full-on grand mal. Poor kid was punching herself in the face and biting her tongue. I ran down to her room, got her on her side, and blocked her from hitting herself in the face during the seizure. I kept her safe and cleaned the blood off of her face from biting her tongue, while I waited to see if she needed rescue meds.

Manny was home at the time, as he hadn't left for work yet. He came down to join us, and while we were lying with her on the bed during her post-ictal state, post seizure, I realized something. I didn't have to run to the bathroom!

I also noticed that my heart rate wasn't racing out of control. As a matter of fact, I didn't feel nervous at all! I immediately felt this was an answer to my prayers that I *needed,* not that I'd wanted. While I always prayed—okay, I begged—for Ava's seizures to be taken away, God took away my fear of them, instead. He didn't cure her epilepsy, but He cured my phobia. How cool is that?

Did this help Ava? In a way, yes. She now has a mom who can help her through some pretty scary times and be fully present, mentally alert, and keep a calm presence for her when she needs it most.

And let me tell you, this relief could not have come at a better time, because the seizures we had seen up until this point were child's play compared to what was to come.

Instinct

I didn't think I had a mother's instinct until the day My People stepped forward. And that moment saved Ava's life.

From day one, Ava has had trouble taking bottles. This was due to her severe hypotonia and having a very poor suck. It took her such a long time to finish one of her bottles because she'd tucker out so many times during the feed. To me, it's probably comparable to trying to keep running when your legs just want to give out.

I tried not to stress over it and instead just appreciate the extra-long time I got to hold her during each feed. A little extra bonding time. You know, me just trying to look at the bright side again, like I did with the whole hydrocephalus hurdle we'd gotten through. I just kept telling myself this was only temporary.

She eventually did gain more strength and was able to start eating some food by mouth. Along with her hypotonia, Ava also didn't have an instinct to chew her foods. Because of that, I started with giving her very watered-down oatmeal. With lots of work and time, she was eventually able to get the chewing technique down and to tolerate eating some stage-3 foods.

Stage-3 foods are baby food with chunks of food in it, so not completely purée̱d. For Ava to reach this stage was no small feat. It was a big moment for both of us! It wasn't easy to get to this point, but she finally started to show some progress after her hard work and also began to enjoy her mealtimes! We were both enjoying her mealtimes, in fact.

Her bottle drinking greatly improved, as well. What had been taking her an hour to drink was now down to about twenty minutes. I even had her drinking some juice and water in between her meals without aspirating, but still using a bottle. Oh, how I had longed for this. It felt amazing!

Ava was in one of her seizure-free periods, and with her mealtimes becoming far less stressful for both of us, I was beyond happy. Once again, I started to get the feeling that the worst was over, and we were on the upswing.

Even though I'd had this feeling before and had it ripped away from me with the onset of her seizures, I was able to forget the past and learn to focus on the now. What happened, happened, right? The now is all I have, and the now had some pretty good things happening, with so much potential! Plus, the way I looked at it was, we had already been through so much, what were the chances of anything bad happening again?

But, like in the past, just when I thought I could start to exhale a little, things did indeed get worse. Ava started to vomit—a lot. If you recall, that is another one of my phobias and a doozy of a phobia.

Just like with her seizures, I couldn't run away from my fear when she vomited, like I had always done my entire life, when anyone threw up. The sound, the smell, the sight, the anticipation of it happening, and the intense fear of it touching me would send me into a full-blown panic.

My normal reaction is to be far enough away from the person so that I could not hear it, smell it, or see it. But, identical to with the seizures, now I was forced to stay. I was forced not just to try to face my fear head-on, but also to be strong enough to help keep Ava feeling safe, comforted, and taken care of. She was *my* responsibility, and she needed me to be strong for her. Man, did that absolutely suck.

It was even harder for me with her not being able to help herself physically at all. She couldn't sit up or lean over, and even if she could, her brain wouldn't know enough to do that. So, just like seizures, if she vomited with no one around her, it could be potentially fatal, if she was not positioned correctly. Not to mention she needed to be positioned to not get it all over herself and all in her hair–been there and done that way too many times.

Through months and months of her vomiting, I took her to see the pediatrician handfuls of times. The doctor tried all kinds of different formulas and medications, assuming it was reflux. None of them worked. We had swallow studies done and appointments with different feeding specialists. Nothing worked, and nothing changed. It just kept getting worse. It was so very frustrating and equally heartbreaking to watch her go through this.

Before the vomiting started, her mealtimes had built up to a point where she would drink her whole bottle in under twenty minutes and eat a whole serving of stage-3 baby food. All in maybe thirty minutes. Now, I am not exaggerating when I say that our entire day was consumed by me feeding her only bottles. She had progressed to throwing up during every single bottle feed, and she would throw up many times during the feed. It would take me maybe an hour just to get her to hold down two ounces total of formula. Drink, puke, drink, puke, cry (me), repeat. All day, all night, every day, every night.

She was also on seizure medication, and she needed to keep those pills in her belly! With those types of medications, you are not allowed any extra number of pills, and you cannot refill any earlier than maybe four days before you run out—because they are controlled substances... Because of that, I had a puppy-training pad on the floor at my feet during her bottle times. I'd lean her forward to throw up on the pad, pick out the seizure meds from the vomit on the pad, wipe them off, and give them to her again.

I called the insurance company over and over, asking for an exception due to what was happening. They didn't care. Ava wasn't seen as a person, only as a number and a liability. They wouldn't budge. It was an extremely stressful time for both of us, and it only got worse.

Over time, Ava soon started to associate bottles with vomiting. She began to refuse to drink at all. She would push her tongue up to the roof of her mouth to try to block me from putting the bottle in her mouth. When I succeeded getting the bottle in her mouth, she'd then cover the nipple of the bottle with her tongue to block the flow of formula. She would just hold her tongue up, pressing firmly, so the bottle couldn't get into her mouth at all. She was completely blocking me from putting it in her mouth. I had to force my finger in her mouth to push her tongue down and try to slip the nipple of the bottle on top of her tongue. This was a lot harder than it sounds. And *very* frustrating.

When I'd finally get her to drink a little, she'd throw it up, and I'd have to start all over again. I'm not going to lie, there were lots of tears from me, many thrown bottles out of frustration—just awful, awful times. I tried as hard as I could to control my frustration, because *she* was the one who was truly suffering. She didn't deserve to think she was upsetting me when she was the one physically going through it, and I was just a bystander. But the way she looked at me when I forced her to eat tore me apart. She didn't know I was trying to help her, not hurt her, but there was no way to explain that to her.

Those months were a blur. I feel like all I did was cry, with several crash-outs thrown into the mix. It was destroying me as a mother, to watch her go through this, especially after also having to deal with seizures and with her being physically and mentally delayed. This just wasn't fair.

At this point, I started to lose my faith in God. I thought, if there truly is a God, how could He just let her suffer like this? Why was He letting this happen to her? She hasn't done anything to deserve this hard life. I may have had some missteps in my own life, but I am, at my core, a kind, caring, person, so what did I do to have this life now? Growing up, it had been drilled into my head that if you are good Christian and follow the rules, God will reward you. So why was I being punished for being good? Why was Ava being punished? I wanted Him to make it make sense.

One day, her vomiting was just… different. It seemed to me to be more like a stomach bug, because she was throwing up when she wasn't eating and more often. Also, she was getting very sweaty, so I assumed she'd had a fever and her body was trying to cool down.

I took Ava to the pediatrician that morning to have her checked out and ask what to do. I took her in because I knew she was already behind on fluids and nutrition, and I had no idea what to do with a stomach bug. Unfortunately, I didn't see her regular pediatrician in the office that day, but instead another physician in the same practice, though we had seen him before.

Knowing Ava's history, he said we were welcome to go get admitted in the hospital in order to get IV fluids into her right then, or we could wait it out. With my fear of ERs and hospitals, I selfishly opted to wait it out. Plus, if it was truly a stomach bug, the vomiting should be slowing down soon. I'd also save her from the chance of picking up something else while she was there and that worried me, given the weakened state she was already in.

He gave me instructions to call if she got worse or if I changed my mind, and they'd let me skip the ER and just start the admission on the pediatrics floor. He was so accommodating to our "special" situation, and I was very grateful for that. In a less-than-perfect situation, it was the perfect plan. It made me feel safe.

So, we went home. Later that afternoon, Ava suddenly looked different to me. Kind of just… flat. I can't explain it any other way. I knew she was sick, I knew she was tired, and I knew she was pale, but something didn't look right. It just didn't feel right.

Something inside of me, for the very first time in her life, *knew* that she needed help and she needed it now.

I called the pediatrician's office, but the awesome doctor I had seen earlier that day had left for the afternoon. Another doctor called me back, someone we had never met; he knew nothing about Ava or her history, and he did not bother to check that before calling me. He didn't even know that we had been in earlier that day or that there was a plan in place to get her admitted.

Our call began with him berating me and asking why I'd waited until the end of the day to call.

I'm sorry, what the ??? I was so taken aback that I didn't know how to react. I'd never been spoken to like that by a doctor. Normally, I would just shrink down and take it. But I knew he was wrong in his assumptions *and* that Ava needed help.

I explained firmly that I certainly did not wait around to call and told him what had happened earlier at the appointment in the office. I was calling him the instant I knew things were getting worse and wanted to start the process for admission. I told him that, unfortunately, Ava's course of illness doesn't watch the clock and didn't care that it was after 4:00 or close to his end of day. Her timeline of her illness progression was out of my control.

To make a very *long* and frustrating story short, he continued to be rude to me, belittle me, and refused to follow the instructions the other doctor left for Ava. He told me to go to the ER and wait in the waiting room like everyone else. Total asshole.

My People, what I call my incredibly strong mother's intuition or gut instincts, totally took over my body and let it be known that they had something to say. I instantly knew Ava didn't have time to sit in the ER. I knew she needed to be admitted *now* and that I was running out of time. I also knew that going to the local hospital wasn't an option for her safety, that Ava needed to go to the hospital up north. I had nothing to back that up, but I was guided by an intense feeling of just *knowing*. I had never felt anything like it before.

I ended up calling Ava's neurologist. Looking back, it makes no sense at all to call her neurologist—what was he going to do? But again, My People took over and were guiding me. I didn't question a thing. I just did what I felt led to do. It was 4:55 p.m. when I reached his secretary by phone, and I begged her to not put me on hold or lose the connection, because at 5:00, I knew the phones would shut down. I would get lost in the phone system, and that terrified me.

Crying, I begged her to find Ava's neurologist and plead with him to admit her. Mind you, he had no idea what has been going on with her vomiting history or what had happened today. I briefly explained what had happened with the asshole pediatrician and that I didn't even want her at the local hospital. She *needed* to be admitted where the pediatric specialists were. My gut told me she needed help that the local hospital could not provide.

She was able to find him and explain to him what was going on, and he asked no questions. I was shocked. He told his secretary to tell us to get in the car immediately and start driving up to the hospital. While we were making the ninety-minute drive up to the hospital, he promised to work on her admission. We would skip the emergency room and head up to the pediatric floor instead.

I will never forget his reason for helping us and admitting her without even seeing her. He stated that while he always trusts a mother's instinct, *mine was so strong,* he not only respected my urgency but made it happen without question.

I drove, while Manny sat in the back with Ava. Our poor little peanut retched the entire ride. I held that steering wheel so tight, with my pedal to the metal, and I never sat back in my seat the entire drive. While it was the fastest that I've ever gotten to that hospital (other than a med flight helicopter ride), it seemed like it took hours. I knew every minute counted, and I hated wasting precious time driving on that highway, trying to get to the hospital.

When we arrived, they didn't have a room ready yet for Ava. They put me in a wheelchair with her on my lap and had us wait in the hallway outside the pediatrics department. While we waited, Ava retched over and over again. Her body was so limp, I was getting more and more frightened, just sitting there, waiting and wasting precious time. It felt like I was losing her, very much like on that day of her very first grand mal seizure.

When they got her in the room, the medical team immediately started trying to put in an IV. It took them over an hour and a half to get the IV in. They had to call in many team members, including several from the NICU team, to place her IV. Ava was so extremely dehydrated, it was nearly impossible to insert an IV into her little vein.

Then they hit me with a stunning confirmation of my mother's instinct I never expected. They told me that Ava's glucose was 27, and if I had waited any longer, she may not have made it.

What?

I was in shock. My People had just saved her life. My incredibly strong instinct, which I had never felt before like this, had actually saved her freaking life. And Ava's neurologist helping to get her admitted equally saved her life, based on my intense intuition. *Woah.* That sure was a lot to take in and process. But My People didn't have time for that, because they were not yet done. They knew it wasn't time to exhale just yet.

The shy, quiet Lisa I had known my entire life, who would never demand anything from anyone, never mind a doctor, was done. She was tired, she was angry, and she was frustrated. But most of all, she was frightened for her daughter and knew, if we went home without resolution, Ava would be in danger.

At that moment, for the first time, I put my foot down and told them I was not leaving this hospital with Ava without her having a feeding tube put in. I was done watching her suffer. I was done with the vomiting. I was done with picking pills out of her vomit. This had been going on far too long, and it was pretty clear her body was over it, too. I wanted our life back. It was time.

And just like that, she was going to get one. They agreed to a gastronomy tube (a G-tube, inserted through a stoma directly into her stomach), and Ava had hers placed within a few days. I felt such immense relief. The stress about getting her proper nutrition and also actually digesting her seizure medications would be gone. Just like that.

I asked the nurse if we could stop the bottle feeds once the G-tube was placed, to give both Ava and me a break. The amount of stress those bottle-feeding sessions had been causing both of us was just too much. What I'd once considered a bonding moment between us became such a negative, hurtful, and dreaded experience for both Ava and myself. Oh, how we both desperately needed a break.

She said that would be no problem at all, that "eating is like riding a bike. She'll get right back to it with no problem."

Hearing that, I felt like the weight I had been carrying just lifted. *Aaaaah.*

Unfortunately, Ava's gut wasn't done being a naughty little piggie. Because, even after the G-tube button was placed, she continued to vomit. She was also still retching. I cannot describe the level of defeat I felt that the G-tube didn't "fix" her issue. I really thought that this nightmare was over for us, and we could go home and get back to a far less stressful life. It also shattered my heart to watch her continue to suffer. It was even harder for her now, since she was also trying to recover from her surgery.

The medical staff didn't understand why the retching and vomiting were still going on, so they did some more tests to take a look inside. They did a barium study from the top down and from the bottom up. They wanted to watch it go through her digestive system to see what happened as she digested her food. Manny and I were both present during the tests, and when the second one was underway, they stopped it suddenly. They told us we were all set and sent us back to the room. Weird.

When we got back to the room, we were met by a surgeon. We were expecting one of the GI team members to come in, not a surgeon. Um, what was happening?

The surgeon began to explain that, during the testing, they found the true reason for the vomiting over the past year. She had a duodenal malrotation of her intestines. The surgeon explained to us that, basically, she was at very high risk of her intestines completely twisting on themselves. They had been flopping back and forth (hence the vomiting and retching), and once the intestines made a full rotation, it could very quickly become, well, in non-medical terms, deadly. And that situation could happen at any moment. Because of that, she was going to require another surgery to repair the malrotation and she was going to need it right away.

This surgery was much longer and much more involved. After the surgeon went in, he discovered that her intestines were all on one side of her body, not across the abdomen like they should have been. They were all kinked up so he had to take them all the way out of her abdomen, fix the malrotation, untwist them, and put them back inside her. After he finished that, he had to move the gastrostomy tube, aka her G-tube, which had just been placed days earlier, to a different part of her stomach.

I remember talking to the doctor and hearing for the first time, "I've never seen anything like that before." At the time, I kind of had an internal giggle, because, as a child growing up, I had heard that a lot about my own body and my different illnesses, so I thought, well, she got it from me. Ha-ha. But unlike my experience, and unfortunately for Ava, the funniness of that statement lost its flair when we ended up hearing it over and over again in future years and in a few more grave situations.

This hospital stay lasted almost four weeks for Ava and me. It was my very first time ever experiencing this type of environment, and for the most part, I was holding up fairly well. Manny stayed at the hospital overnight and then got up super-early to drive back down to work in another state. He'd drive about four hours a day to see us while he was also working full days. I was more worried about him than me.

I was just sitting in a hospital room, watching TV all day and chilling with Ava. I had it pretty good, I thought. Oh, how I want to go back to myself in that moment right now and smack myself on the side of the head. Having it pretty good turned out to be the furthest thing from the truth. I'd eventually find out the hard way just how much those hospital stays were affecting me.

During this hospital stay, Ava had lots of tests done. We had previously scheduled an outpatient spinal tap and brain MRI, which were coming up in the next month, so I asked, since we were there, could we get those done during our stay. The spinal tap was part of the many, many tests done to find a diagnosis for her. The brain MRI was to redo the one ordered by her first neurologist, the one who'd said she was "fine." Her current neurologist wanted to get another MRI done with more detail. She also had blood drawn for different genetic tests and the like.

When young children have tests like MRIs, they are sedated. That is because you cannot expect them to stay still during the test. That and it is extremely loud and would be scary for a child to go through. But in Ava's case, during this hospital stay, they didn't feel comfortable sedating her again in her condition. My People weren't having that, so I asked if it would be okay if I held her head steady during the MRI, to forgo the sedation. They had never been presented with that question or had anyone actually do that, but they were on board to try it.

Um, what the heck did I just sign myself up for? I am claustrophobic. How was I going to survive being in an MRI tube for starters, never mind with another body? My People didn't have time to think about these things, though. They were just thinking about Ava and what was right for her in the moment. So, I just went with it.

Turns out, I am capable of doing a lot of very hard, unimaginable things when it comes to Ava (and in the future, for my twins, too). I just somehow do whatever needs to be done. No fear, no worries, no second guessing. I just do it. So, for her MRI, she lay on her back, and I lay on top of her, holding her head firmly. We were nose to nose in that MRI tunnel for the entire series of scans.

Somehow, someway, I was able to focus only on why I was doing what I was doing and to push down any negative thoughts I had. It felt a little bit empowering to be able to do that. It made me feel like a supermom! I had silently struggled when we didn't have our initial bond, but now, after facing not one, but two of my major phobias head on, I overcame another by dealing with the claustrophobia. Actually, three phobias because, well, emergency rooms!

I still very much had those fears and phobias, but for some reason, when it came to Ava, I could not only get over the "I've *got* to get out of here right now" feeling, but it was as if I could run toward the fear. Maybe I was a good mom after all, I thought.

But was I overcoming my fears or just beginning to master the art of "pushing it down"? Only time would tell.

Even though the situation I was in was ridiculously different than any other moms I knew, I finally started to feel like "one of the gang." I was beginning to feel like I fit in as a mother. I was developing some serious confidence about how I navigated this world, raising Ava, and it felt so good. And I felt ready to face anything, because, after experiencing how things just unfolded due to my unknown and freakishly spot-on motherly instincts, I knew we were going to be okay. Life was hard, but we were going to be okay. This brought me a little bit of peace in my not-so-peaceful world.

It was easy for me to be positive during that hospital stay, because, like I mentioned, Manny stayed with me every night. (Our twins were not yet born.) Also, my parents visited every other day and brought me Dunkin' Donuts' iced coffee and snacks when they made the trip up. When they weren't visiting, they were taking care of our dog and cat at home, making sure Manny had things to eat there, as well as keeping up with the laundry for us. They were so amazing, helping us. Talk about feeling supported, loved, and cared for. I was so lucky to have them.

Thank God my parents were at the hospital visiting when we found out the results of Ava's MRI. I will never forget that moment when her neurologist told us what was going on. We all stood at the nurse's station—me, Manny, my mom, and my dad—while the neurologist explained to us that Ava's brain had developed differently: congenital cerebral cortical dysgenesis, polymicrogyria, white-matter abnormalities, and corpus callosum syndrome…

As he was showing what her brain looked like us on the computer screen, he pointed to the areas that were issues. He said, "See that? That's not supposed to be there." Over and over again.

Even though what he was saying was so extremely hard to hear, what made it unforgettable and even more painful was that he said it with a tear in his eye. He was probably going through something in his own life, but man, seeing him like that tore at my heart. He must have sensed my emotions and my bazillion questions and put his hand on my shoulder.

"Sometimes, all you can do is just love her."

Fuck. Those words created so much dread, defeat, and doom inside of me. While we were surrounded by the sounds and movement of the hustle and bustle of a busy pediatrics inpatient floor, I didn't hear a thing, and I didn't notice anyone. I felt completely alone. I felt detached from life in that moment.

I now knew my dreams of a fixable condition or curable diagnosis were not going to happen. The things that I had prayed to God for over and over were not going to happen. The diagnosis and cure that I thought would become the purpose of my life and the reason for Ava's suffering were not going to happen. Every single thing I had prayed for was not going to happen. Ava would never get better. Our lives would always be a struggle. That moment changed my life forever.

After receiving that information, I had to go back into Ava's hospital room, see her smiling face, and try to act like nothing had happened, like nothing changed. It was not her fault that this had happened to her, so I certainly couldn't let my feelings affect her. She was the one who was suffering. I was just the one watching it. She should be the one who is upset, not me.

She was the one who had just had two surgeries and was puking her guts out for months. She was the one who felt the seizures and endured unspoken pain. She was the one who couldn't do anything without complete assistance. If anyone should be upset, it was her. Yet, there she was, the happiest human I have ever met. Smiling away in her crib with tubes coming out of her. She hadn't left the room in almost a month, other than for tests, yet was acting like life is good.

Just like I learned to push down my fear during the MRI, I started to learn how to push down my pain in order to be strong for Ava. I made a promise to myself that I would never, ever allow my fears, my sadness, or my frustrations about her medical issues affect her in any way. If she could smile at me in the toughest of times, then I'd be damned if I couldn't smile back.

Ava was taking a long time to heal post-malrotation surgery, much longer than anyone had anticipated. Her digestive system took a lot longer to wake up than what is typical, and that kept us from being discharged. Her insides were still pretty pissed off from that surgery. Because of that, those spinal tap results that we were supposed to get at a follow-up appointment after her discharge? Yeah, they came in while we were inpatient at the hospital.

What they found was that Ava had an extremely low level of 5-methyltetrahydrofolate in her spinal fluid. 5-methyltetrahydrofolate, or 5-MTHF for short, is needed for lots of neurological functions. Because of this finding, Ava was diagnosed with Cerebral Folate Deficiency Syndrome. The symptoms of this condition, CFD, are developmental delay, seizures, hypotonia, speech issues, and more—all of which Ava has! The best news about it was there is a treatment for this condition, and if it was her true diagnosis, a dramatic recovery could be possible.

Once again, after hitting such a blow with the MRI results, thinking our lives would never improve, I was given the chance to believe there could still be a glimmer of hope. There was a huge possibility of us not just finding out what had been wrong with her, but even of her gaining some skills. With treatment from a drug called Leucovorin, which is folinic acid, some kids had started talking and walking, their seizures diminished, and their lives were dramatically improved. It sounded almost too good to be true.

At the time, Cerebral Folate Deficiency was very rare. So rare that only a handful of kids worldwide had been diagnosed with it. That meant there was not a lot of information on it, and because of that, lots of kids and families were not getting the proper diagnosis. Without having their cerebral spinal fluid tested, there is no way to know this could be going on in their bodies. I was informed that a lot of kids received a diagnosis of cerebral palsy or just developmental delay when they actually could have Cerebral Folate Deficiency. Because of this, they were missing out on a potentially life-changing treatment.

I was trying not to jump ahead, but holy shitballs, this fit everything I had been hoping and praying for! Ava could potentially have a miraculous turnaround in her delays, despite what the MRI showed. And... since Cerebral Folate Deficiency is so rare, it would need to be talked about more, awareness would be needed, and families would need to be educated about it. *THIS WAS GOING TO BE HER CURE AND MY PURPOSE*! I could feel it!

We were told, if this was indeed the root cause of all of Ava's issues and her primary diagnosis, she would show an improvement pretty quickly, once she started the medication. I could not wait to get her on it, so we started immediately, while she was still in the hospital. She didn't show any changes while we were there, but she was only on it for a few days before we got discharged.

We finally went home in the last week of May. It was such a magical time for me. I remember being in awe of how much had changed in our yard during those weeks in the hospital. Spring was bringing so many things back to life—things were blooming and full of promise. I felt like it was a sign for me that my life and Ava's life were also about to come back to life and bloom. What an absolutely incredible feeling it was to have just gone through such a difficult first two years of her life and now to have the possibility of not only finding treatment but also to be able to pay it forward with awareness for other families.

I was on top of the world. I felt so much stronger after what I had gone through. I felt grateful for what I'd experienced because it gave me that strength and the confidence to trust my instincts and to know I really am not just a good mom, but a freaking bad-ass one! Life was feeling so good.

When we got home, I had plans of us getting back to the place we had left off with eating before all of this puking stuff started. That now she would be able to have fun with food and get the nutrition she needed through the G-tube. Like she could have yummy snacks by mouth or chocolate or ice cream! The nurse had said it was like riding a bike and that our three-week break of her taking nothing by mouth would have no effect on her eating. I couldn't wait for her to erase the negativity she had around eating and replace it with the pleasures of so many good foods she had been missing out on!

But the thing we'd both over looked was that Ava is "different." Her brain works differently than ours, and it turns out she never did get back on that bike. I don't think her brain even remembered riding a bike at all.

The act of firmly placing her tongue at the roof of her mouth never went away. It would be a learned behavior that she would never be able to unlearn. No more opening her mouth for a spoon, for a bottle, for a cup, for a toothbrush, or for chocolate. Not even after years of therapies, years of facial massages, and years of me working with her every single day. Not even after a trip to a feeding clinic down in Baltimore. Her brain could not ever let go of the protection mechanism it developed, blocking anything from entering her mouth.

After almost a decade of trying every single day to get her to eat, I finally decided to stop, to throw in the towel. No more trying to force her to do something she truly didn't want to do. Sure, it broke my heart that she was missing out on so much joy and pleasure from the tastes of different foods, but even with that I decided to stop. Some battles are worth fighting for, but this one got the white flag from me. There was no need to keep pushing her when she clearly didn't want to do it. Poor kid had enough to stress about in her life.

So, since she was getting her full nutrition from her tube feeds and we were able to administer her meds so they got properly absorbed, that was enough for me. With all of our other daily struggles, it was actually quite a relief to let something go. We didn't often find closure for things in Ava's life, so this was definitely a welcome closure for us.

She may have been losing something that most of us love, but she was gaining so much more. The malrotation surgery and the G-tube ultimately led us to being able to quiet one of the most stressful daily battles Ava and I had faced for years. I'd call that a win. Heartbreak aside, a win is a win.

Without Her

She taught me everything - except how to live without her. And suddenly, I had three little humans who needed me to figure it out.

For my entire life, even after getting married and having Ava, I always turned to my mother for advice and guidance. I mean, mothers know best, right? No matter what situation I was facing, she always knew what to do. Whether it was knowing what I should wear to an event, what temperature to cook chicken at or when she thought it was time to call the doctor for Ava. She was like my own walking, talking personal Google search.

She had also always been there for me for everything in my life. I mean *everything*. We went through our normal four-ish years of battles during my teenage angst, ha-ha. Not too many mother/daughter relationships can make it through those years without lots of drama. It's like a rite of passage. After the teen terrors were over, we became best friends again. Shopping, coffees, laughing, finishing each other's sentences, binging TV shows, sneaking cigarette breaks, and sunbathing—total besties.

When I say I turned to my mother for advice and guidance, it wasn't just once in a while. It was every damn day. I don't think I ever made a decision that didn't involve me running it by her. I needed to know if she thought it was a good idea or if I was making the right decision. I always thought this was because I valued her opinion, but now, years after her passing, I see it differently. I can see now that I wanted… okay, let's be honest, *needed* her approval, because I was afraid of to make a decision she didn't agree with.

Now, before I go any further, I have to say up front that my mother was absolutely *amazing.* She was very kind, giving, caring, and she was truly my very best friend. I loved her so very much and still do. That being said, anything she did or said to me was never with any negative intent.

I won't get into her life story because that is not my story to tell. I know she was very determined that I have a successful life and not go through any hardships or experience an ounce of any of the pain she endured growing up, as I sought to achieve my dreams. The way she went about making sure of this was to block me from making any decisions she felt might jeopardize my peace or future success. She would not let me fail, but to ensure that, she definitely let me know when she didn't agree with something that could potentially lead me to pain or failure.

What most don't know about me is that I despise confrontation. I will do anything and everything in my power to avoid conflict. The thought of getting into an argument with someone terrifies me. While I was not lacking in confidence, I never wanted to hurt anyone's feelings. So, to confront someone could mean possibly making them angry or ending up in an argument. Nope, not gonna happen. I can see now just how damaging that approach can be, but throughout my life, I truly thought it was my only option. Avoid confrontation = avoid pain.

That being said, if my mom didn't "approve" of a decision I was making, from a potential date to choosing a career or even picking an outfit to wear to a wedding, she was not subtle about her disapproval. I'd get the stare, the silent treatment, and basically, she would not let up until I did things *her* way. She made it quite uncomfortable for me, knowing how much I wanted her approval and to avoid any dreaded confrontations. I can see now she was doing the best she could in the only way she knew how, so again, no shade to her at all.

When Manny and I looked to purchase our first home, my parents wanted us to move into a house with an in-law apartment attached. I thought that was an amazing idea, since my mom was my bestie. Also, even though Manny and I didn't have kids yet, I envisioned built-in babysitters and/or daycare for us in the future. Total win/win for everyone.

While they had their own in-law apartment, the washer and dryer were located in my basement and shared among us. That meant, whenever she wanted to do any laundry, she'd have to come over to my house to do it. Because of that, she said it was easier to do all of our laundry at once. How convenient, right? Ha-ha! She happily washed, dried, and folded all of our laundry. But it didn't stop there.

When Ava started having her medical issues, she also cooked a lot of our meals for us and hung with me and Ava all day, like *all* day, *every* day. In the morning, we had coffee together at my house, then we'd have lunch at hers, and played upstairs with Ava on her "big bed" in the afternoon. Mom would bring dinner over for me and Manny to eat lots of times, and we'd watch Red Sox games together at night at her house. Oh, how I miss those days.

I honestly don't know how I could have made it through those years without her. She was still very judgmental of my decisions, but she was also a shoulder for me to cry on. She was my copilot at Ava's doctors' appointments, my confidant, and my escape. She was my rock. When she passed away suddenly in 2010, when Ava was almost seven, I felt like my whole world was ripped away from me. I not only lost my mother, but I lost my everything. We'd been together every day, all day, and now, I was suddenly alone.

No more going next door to ask if I should give Ava Tylenol or Motrin for fever. No asking if she thought I was seeing a seizure. No one to ask if I could escape and take a car ride, because I felt like I was losing it. No one to watch Red Sox games with. No one to talk to. No more emotional support. No more hugs. No more rock. No more ride-or-die.

Yes, I was married, and yes, Manny should have been all of those things. In a perfect world, he would have been. But, to be honest, lots of times, we have struggled in our marriage. Special needs parents have a much higher rate of divorce, and I am sure you can figure out why. Having Ava as our first child took a definite toll on us. And even though we lived together, one time we barely spoke to each other for three whole years. Not many people knew about that because, well, it's personal and between me and Manny. It was one of those things I kept silent about and just pushed down inside. We couldn't change our situation, so it was something I'd just have to deal with.

April 26, 2010 was the first day in my entire life when I woke up and every decision I made now had to be on my own. I felt like a castaway lost at sea. How would I know what temperature the oven needed to be for my recipe? What kind of gifts should I get Ava's therapists for

Christmas? What do these symptoms that Ava is having mean? What doctor do I call? Do I go to the ER? Mom? *Mom? Mom…*

Saying that everything changed for me when my mother passed is an understatement. My entire life changed. For the first time in Ava's life, I was alone with her. No one to watch her while I ran to the bathroom or when I took a shower or even when I needed to run out to the store. I was still very much afraid of seizures and, let me tell you, still afraid to use her rescue med, Diastat. I think I was more afraid of that than of the seizure. Plus, to administer Diastat, you have to inject it in the rectum. Can you imagine being in the middle of Walmart and having to put your kid on the gross, dirty floor and pull their pants down to inject this, all while they are having a seizure? Yeah, *much* easier to stay home. When I had my mom around, I always had a second set of hands. That guidance, assistance, and security was all gone, after she passed.

I very easily could have spiraled into another depression. I had suffered from depression about a year prior to my mother's passing, when I was trying to deal with the life I had lost, the life I currently was living, and my life looking into the future. I didn't want this life. I didn't want to be at home, I didn't want to be shut off from society, and I didn't want to have to see and deal with the things I did. It was a very dark place to be in, and depression won.

Luckily, I was able to find a medication on the second try that helped me tremendously with my mental health. Being on that medication and the fact that I was able to get approval from my mother for something weighing heavy on my heart before she passed were what kept me going.

That something that weighed heavily on my heart was about having any more children. I had poured my heart out to my mother in March, just a month before she passed, about how I was turning forty later on that year and starting to panic about Ava's future. About things like who would care for her if something happened to me or Manny? Who would be a voice for her when she couldn't speak? Who could lift her, if something physically happened to us and we couldn't?

I didn't want to ask my family, because that would put them into a very uncomfortable position. If I struggled with raising Ava, who was my own kid, how would someone else want to willingly take on that burden? I also didn't want someone to place her in an institution or care facility, since that is what would probably happen. It's not easy to give up your entire life for Ava's care and well-being. I would never expect that of someone else, nor would I think anyone actually would. So, my brain went to the next best option. A sibling, which meant another baby.

I had been too afraid to even consider having any other children for a few reasons. First, I was turning forty. Not the best age to be trying for another baby, but even more so in my situation. The older you are at conception, the higher the chance of problems and complications.

Second, Ava still had no primary diagnosis. She has a handful of things wrong with her, but not one main diagnosis that causes it all. No root cause. Without a diagnosis, we'd have no idea if whatever happened to her would happen again to another baby. I would have been beyond devastated if I brought another child into the world who would struggle so much.

Not to mention how heartbreaking and utterly stressful it would be, as a mother, to have to raise two children like that. What would I do if, let's say, I was bathing a baby and Ava had a seizure and I was alone? I can't just leave the baby in the tub, and I can't just leave Ava seizing. What would happen if I had to stay in the hospital, and we didn't have anyone to watch our baby while Manny worked? Lots of what-ifs, because we had been through so much already.

But during that conversation with my mother, I was actually quite surprised when she said she welcomed the idea of another child. She said she'd love to help me with the baby and how wonderful it would be for Ava to have a sibling and a playmate. Ava could see what it's like when typical kids hit their milestones, and maybe by seeing that, it would help her learn how to do it herself.

My mom also wanted me to get to experience a typical pregnancy and the natural birth I had wanted with Ava. She talked about how the baby could actually help me as he/she grew and eventually, hopefully, be willing to be the advocate I dreamed of for Ava, when Manny and I were not able.

I was in total awe. I had so many reasons not to have another child, but my mom was really on board with it. Blew my mind! I thought she'd be saying how there was no way I could do that with all I currently had on my plate. She had said that very thing to me over and over again, whenever I'd suggested I wanted to "work" from home. So, to hear her say that a baby was something she was on board with was completely unexpected and pretty freaking awesome!

She actually gave me a glimmer of hope. Hope that I could get to experience what other mothers did with their "typical" kiddos and that, while things were hard for me now, someday they would be much easier.

I began thinking of a future where I'd be able to hear little baby babbles, the sound of giggles, but especially the sound of little bare feet running around inside the house. To see Ava interacting with and playing with her sibling. How beautiful would that be? I had never even considered being able to experience those things in my life until now. I had just blocked them out of my mind.

And the best part was, I'd get to experience them with my mom. I am sure she wanted to see me experience all of that after what she'd seen me go through. What incredible feelings of hope, of joy, and of excitement I was able to feel again. I couldn't wait!

That led me to talk to Manny about adding to our little family, and he was immediately on board. Had we not had Ava, he said he would have wanted to fill up our house with kids. OMG. I was exploding with excitement! Holy shit… It was really happening. We were going to try for another baby!

I even got as far as talking about baby names with my mom. We planned to start trying that summer, after we could get a maternity rider added to Manny's insurance. But that excitement about the future, which I had lost in the six years caring for Ava, just left me when my mom passed. Me and Ava were all alone now.

We lost our sidekick, our playmate, and our bestie. There was absolutely no way I could have another baby without help and support from my mom. To say I was crushed was an understatement. The quietness of her absence in my house, the reassurance from her that it would still be okay, started to lead me down that dark and hopeless path. In her passing was when I needed her most and she was the furthest away from me. I was quickly on my way to losing myself again to depression. The saying, "My mother taught me everything except how to live without her" definitely summed up how I felt.

Months later, I woke up one morning and thought, "Maybe I *can* do this." Sure, it was scary, sure it was risky, but what if it somehow all worked out? What if I actually had a healthy baby? What if facing my fear and having a baby really could help Ava to hit her own milestones? What if they found a diagnosis for her while I was pregnant, got her treated, and we'd all just ride off into the sunset like some corny Hallmark movie?

I mean, it *could* happen.

For the first time since I had Ava, I could actually *visualize* it happening. Also, for the first time, I had true hope. Hope for a chance at a normal life, to be able to complain about the things other mothers complain about, like hearing, "Mom. Mom. Mom," over and over or having no personal space and never peeing along again. I would no longer feel out of place in mom groups or when with friends when they talked about all the things their kids were doing. I would feel like I was part of the world again. I could be just a mom to her child, not also a caregiver.

Our first pregnancy resulted in a loss. I soon became pregnant again, but because of the prior loss and because of my age (making mine a geriatric pregnancy with a due date at forty years old—insert eye roll...), they wanted me to have an ultrasound done early, to be sure the pregnancy was viable.

The night before the ultrasound, I had a dream, one of those clear-as-day dreams. Throughout my life, I have had many of them. They ended up being sort of like premonitions. So, when I had this one, even though it was "just a dream," it certainly got my attention as a possible peek at what was to come.

In that dream, we went to the ultrasound, and there were two babies on the monitor. Twins! I remember thinking that was more of a nightmare, because *what*? *Twins*? Scary AF, but I secretly hoped the dream was real. Scary, but how cool would that be?

While at breakfast the next morning, sitting at the kitchen table with Manny, I told him about my dream. He knows about my dreams and how they can sometimes predict things, but he just laughed at this one. That put my mind at ease a bit. So, we both laughed—Twins? Us? Ha-ha-ha-ha. Thank God it was just a dream, we thought.

When we were at the ultrasound, we didn't say anything to the technician, because we honestly didn't think having twins was a possibility. Plus, she might think I was a complete lunatic because, to an outsider, I am positive that's what I would have sounded like!

All we really wanted to see on this ultrasound was a sack with a little bean in it and a heartbeat. When we looked up at the screen and it clearly showed *two* sacks and *two* little beans with *two* little heartbeats, Manny and I were stunned. Twins, indeed.

Our reaction externally was not of shock or amazement, and probably appeared nonchalant. I then told the technician about my dream, and she was flabbergasted. But now it made sense to her that we were not totally freaking out or caught off guard, because my dream kind of lessened the shock. Trust me, we were *very* surprised, but somehow the dream took away some of that *OMG WE ARE HAVING TWINS* mentality—ha-ha.

But when we left and Manny went off to work, my brain went into overdrive. How could we afford two more babies with me not working? Manny was now self-employed, we had private, ridiculously expensive health insurance, and he was our only source of income. Double the diapers, the cribs, the clothes, the formula and highchairs, etc. How could I do this without the physical and emotional support of my mom being next door? I'd have no one to help out with double the feedings, double the diaper changes, and *still* have to take care of Ava and her medical needs and tube feeds. Manny would probably need to work longer days, so I'd have to do this all alone, all day, every day. If I struggled with just Ava, how could I do this? But there was no turning back now…

Then there was the bigger fear of what if they have issues like Ava? Because Ava still had no diagnosis, I opted out of prenatal testing, because nothing would show anyway. I didn't want to risk the twins' cozy little home in my belly for unnecessary tests that really wouldn't give me any information. Plus, even if something were to be found, I wouldn't be terminating the pregnancy, so it just didn't justify the risk.

My pregnancy was one of the hardest things for me to go through mentally up to that point, and I am sure it was for Manny, as well. Every ultrasound, every stress test, watching for issues, and waiting for our luck to run out the further I got into the pregnancy. It was nine months of not knowing and praying for the best situation while also mentally preparing for the possibility of the worst situation.

My mentality since having Ava has been to prepare for the worst but hope for the best.

The good news: my pregnancy, even though high risk for my maternal age and because of Ava, was almost perfect. I had planned on having the natural birth I'd wanted with Ava, even though it was twins. I wanted to experience it all and feel it all, totally drug free.

And I was going to get my wish, until my son, Desmond flipped in the final month of my pregnancy. With my being on the smaller side, you can just imagine there really wasn't a heck of a lot of room for two babies in those final weeks, never mind the space for him to flip back.

Because of that, I had to have a C-section. Sigh.

I remember lying on the table after the C-section, asking over and over, "Are they okay? Are they healthy? Are they going to the NICU?"

I couldn't believe it when they not only didn't get whisked off to the NICU like lots of twins do, but they were two completely healthy babies! As a matter of fact, Jillian was able to hit a milestone in her first few hours of life that took Ava over five months to do—lift her head! I just knew at that moment with all certainty that they were both going to be just fine.

We did it. Manny and I did it. Jillian and Desmond had arrived perfect in every way. We successfully created two healthy, little, built-in besties for Ava to love her, to play with her, to grow up with her, to help her, to be her future voice, and to take the fear away Manny and I carried about Ava's care in the future.

I was equally proud, excited, and relieved. And for the first time since my mom passed away, I was optimistic.

Sure, our life was going to be incredibly hard for us for many years to come, but knowing that Ava was going to be taken care of by people who love her until her last days is worth anything we had to face.

I'm sure my mom was looking down at us from Heaven with the biggest smile on her face.

The Perfect Storm

Nothing was random.
Every small thing stacked into something bigger.
And that was the moment I understood: no one knew Ava better than I did.

Up until now, whenever I heard someone mention "the perfect storm," I assumed they were talking about the movie with Mark Wahlberg and George Clooney in it. I have never watched it myself, but I know it has to do with the ocean, fishermen, and a vicious Nor'easter, otherwise known as a "wicked-bad storm" to us New England-ahs. Ha-ha.

Something about the ocean absolutely terrifies me. I get shivers just thinking about what those men must have seen, heard, and endured aboard that boat, facing that gigantic storm. Nope, no need for me to watch that.

I had no idea I would learn, through my own personal experience, that a perfect storm isn't just a movie. It can also be, according to Webster's dictionary, "a critical or disastrous situation created by a powerful concurrence of factors."

Yup, in my case, what was supposed to have been a special time for our little growing family, full of hope, excitement, and normalcy, turned out to be one of the most difficult seasons we ever went through. Ava's accumulation of medical incidents created her "perfect storm," something she would need to weather for a decade more.

Looking back, I can see how this season didn't just change Ava's medical history. It quietly rewired how I mothered, how I trusted doctors, and how I trusted myself.

It all started in the fall of 2010 with a positive pregnancy test. Ava was seven years old at the time.

As soon as we were in the clear and had maternity coverage on our insurance, we'd started trying for a baby right away. I was thirty-nine and had been told, as women age, it becomes more difficult to become pregnant. We had no time to waste, because what also happens as women age is the chances for issues with the pregnancy, baby, and mom also go up. I ain't got time for that!

Thinking that it'd be a struggle, I was prepared. I had thermometers, ovulation kits, charts—all the things. I was ready for the long haul, so it was a total shock that I got pregnant during the first month of trying. What a relief! It felt so good to have crossed one potential issue off our list. I actually could still get pregnant as a crotchety, aging dinosaur without any help needed. *Phew.*

I started to have pregnancy symptoms right out of the gate—bouts of nausea, exhaustion, lightheadedness. I wasn't upset about the nausea because I actually kind of wanted to experience morning sickness. I know that sounds crazy, but hear me out. If you recall, I didn't get to have a normal pregnancy with Ava, nor have anything typical after her birth.

This time, I wanted to feel all the things that other moms did. Again, I wanted to feel included along with other moms and be able to join in the conversations about all of the things I didn't experience during my pregnancy with

Ava. Even if it meant nausea and potentially throwing up, I wanted to go through it.

All was well until our first ultrasound. There was a sac but no baby. *Huh*? That didn't make sense. I had all of the symptoms. They said sometimes it can happen and had us come back for another ultrasound a week later. Maybe the baby was just hiding and would show at the next one. Nope, once again, just a sac, no baby. They said it's called a blighted ovum, and even though my body thinks it is pregnant, it is not. *No baby*? *What*? It didn't make sense, because I felt pregnant. It was like a cruel joke.

Once again, we'd begun to feel hope and joy and then, *BAM,* it was gone. I was crushed. This wasn't part of the plan. I'd been planning on potential issues *getting* pregnant, but not *being* pregnant.

I opted for a D&C rather than the option of taking the medication to pass the non-viable pregnancy at home. It was the better option for my body, since we wanted to try again right away. I also didn't want to pass it on my own, because honestly, with my luck, Ava would end up in the hospital or something, and I'd have to be there with her while actively miscarrying. I always had to prepare for the worst, because our track record wasn't so good about getting through stuff without issues.

When I made that choice, I didn't yet know that the D&C was done in the ob-gyn's office. Looking back, I can see just how barbaric that was. They gave me a shot of Advil in my butt cheek right before the procedure, and *that was it*. OMG. I have a pretty high pain tolerance, but even with that, I let out a big loud scream during the procedure… Okay, at one point, F-bombs. If you ever need to have a D&C done, do *not* have it done in the doctor's office. Definitely get sedated… I'd say it was like getting a cavity filled without Novocain. It was that bad.

After overcoming that hurdle, as soon as we got the green light to try again, we did. And once again, I got that positive pregnant test on the first try. Just call me Fertile Myrtle, I guess. As you already know, this time it I had a viable pregnancy but still not "normal." Nope! I'd be a forty-year-old mother to twins. That made me high risk, due to my "advanced maternal age" and due to my carrying multiples, even more so as that crotchety old-ass dinosaur mother carrying twins.

I never worried, though. Not one bit. Something told me everything was going to be fine, especially knowing what I had experienced before. I promised those little beans I'd take the best care of them in their little rental units. I wanted them to be healthy. I *needed* them to be healthy. Ava also needed them to be healthy.

Let me tell you, twins bring a whole lot of hormones with them from day one. The exhaustion was intense, and I gave up caffeine for the beanies' safety, so staying awake was a struggle and a half. As I was just trying to survive each day, I often thought how the heck would I be able to handle any sort of medical stuff with Ava. I couldn't imagine. I hoped I didn't need to find out.

Our first medical hurdle during the pregnancy started when Manny was playing with Ava. He was always spinning her around and playing "airplanes" with her, making her giggle and squeal with joy. He would also help her with her standing and freestanding, and she loved that. She always looked so stinking proud of herself. In one of those play sessions, when he put her into standing, he forgot to put on her AFO braces first.

Because she had no brace, she had no support for her lower legs, ankles, and feet, but especially for the backs of her feet. I didn't know this at the time, but when children are growing, the backs of their feet are still cartilage and don't turn into bone until their mid-teens. Isn't that fascinating?

When Ava got tired of standing, or maybe if she just didn't want to do it anymore, she would buckle her knees to release from standing up. But when she did it this particular time, she ended up tearing the cartilage in the backs of both feet. Without the braces on, she didn't have the stability the braces gave her. Since she was only seven, her bone wasn't fully formed, either, and it tore easily. Ouch.

When I got her into the orthopedist, she said Ava would need to wear casts on her feet for the injuries to heal. Both feet casted at the same time, and Ava would not be able to do any weight-bearing while the feet were healing. That isn't good for a growing child, having no weight-bearing, but it had to be done in order for her to heal.

I didn't argue with it, because honestly, I was so tired, I had no energy to educate myself on it or question it at all. Not sure if it was the hormones or the exhaustion, but My People weren't speaking up, so I just went along with the plan.

No one mentioned to me that when a child doesn't bear weight, they are at risk for developing kidney stones. Without bearing weight on their growing bones, they end up releasing more calcium into the bloodstream, which leads to the formation of kidney stones. They should also increase their water intake to prevent the formation of the stones. Even though Ava already had a kidney stone and was at a higher risk of developing more, no one told me this information or made sure we were taking precautions. Keep this in mind for later on.

Ava ended up making it through the whole casting fiasco, which ended up taking a total of over two months. We were about to start getting her back into standing when she caught a stomach bug.

Stomach bugs for kids who take seizure medications are extremely stressful. It is so difficult to deal with the vomiting alone, but even harder to keep track of what meds went in and when and what meds came out and when. I had to be sure to note the time her meds were given, so I could figure about how long they were in her system. I'd know how much of her medicine was absorbed, if she happened to throw up around med times, so I could then estimate what dosage I had to readminister. It feels like I'm a mad scientist at times.

I also had to space them out and give them one at a time between throw-ups. Then, measure out the volume of sips or milliliters of formula and free water, to keep track of her hydration levels, as well as tracking her urine output. All while pregnant and just trying to survive the days.

A stomach bug, as you know, can cause dehydration fairly quickly and very easily in children. And what can dehydration cause? Kidney stones. Did I know that? No. No one told me that. Again, hold onto that thought for later on.

Did I mention all of this happened during the holiday season, and I still hadn't told anyone I was pregnant? I was still doing all of the Christmas stuff—shopping for family, sending Christmas cards, decorating, and activities with Ava's school, gifts for teachers and therapists. Trying to act "normal," when I was growing two humans who were seemingly sucking the life out of me!

We got through the holidays, but there was no time to exhale and start to enjoy the pregnancy. Nope. When I was eleven weeks pregnant, I woke up to go to the bathroom in the middle of the night, and I saw something I'd never expected: the entire toilet was filled with blood. Blood was everywhere. It was pouring out of me. I felt no pain, but this had to be a miscarriage. OMG. I was losing these little beanies. *NO*! Not again. I couldn't do this again.

I started screaming for Manny that I needed help. He was dead asleep in the bed just outside the bathroom. I told him there was blood everywhere and that I thought I was losing the babies. I was freaking out big time. I was shaking all over in fear, with tears rolling down my cheeks, because I couldn't bear to go through a loss again.

I'm not sure if he wasn't fully awake or thought I was acting like a lunatic because of the hormones. Maybe he didn't truly understand that the bathroom looked like a crime scene. But he just yelled back, asking me if I needed to go to the ER. He didn't come into the bathroom. He kept falling back asleep. Man, I wish I had his superpowers to fall asleep that fast. It is absolute sorcery!

At one point he said, if I was passing the babies, he couldn't do anything about it, anyway. I mean, in reality, he isn't wrong. But I'm not sure he totally grasped what was actually going on. I think, if he'd seen it, he may have had a different suggestion.

I had no idea what to do. Man, did I need my mom.

I ended up quietly cleaning up the mess, got some towels and some puppy training pads to lie on in the bed, and figured, he's right. If I went to the ER, I'd have to drive myself, because he had to stay home with Ava, then go through all of that potentially devastating testing and bad news all alone. What difference did it make if I went now or in the morning? It would be the same outcome. I wanted to just lie down, hold my belly, and potentially enjoy my last night together with my two little babies. So, I just went to bed and softly cried myself to sleep.

That night, I realized I could be married and still feel completely alone in a moment that terrified me.

The next morning, the three of us headed to the Ob-Gyn's office. Turned out, I had a subchorionic hemorrhage. I was not losing the babies! They were still very much there, still growing, and had strong heartbeats. I will never comprehend how a human body can bleed that much and be okay. I did go back a few days later for them to recheck, and all was good. But with it being twins, I had the potential to be put on bed rest in the future. That was *not* an option since I was the fulltime caregiver for Ava. She was completely dependent on me for everything.

Here we go again, I thought. Same cycle. Once again, we are never able to fully be excited for something or experience something without some sort of traumatic event or a fear of something going horribly wrong. There was no way I could ever go on bed rest. We didn't have a backup plan for that, so it just couldn't happen. But there was no time for pity parties or any more worrying, because I had babies to grow *and* a kitchen remodel to finish...

Before I get into the kitchen, there was one more out-of-the-ordinary event with Ava during this time I was carrying the twins. She had been a little low in her alkaline phosphatase the last few times it was checked. Nothing majorly concerning, and My People didn't really seem bothered at all. Her metabolic neurologist had wanted to add in a zinc supplement, but I kept saying no. I hated adding anything more to her medications and supplements, because she was taking so much already. I feel like, if she doesn't absolutely need it, I don't want to give it to her. But I finally caved when both the nutritionist and the metabolic neurologist suggested it again.

They wanted to bring up her alkaline phosphatase by giving her a high dose of zinc for a short time. It wasn't permanent, so I figured why not just get it done. We went ahead and gave it to her because both specialists thought it would be quite beneficial for her. They told me it would be fine with all of her other medications and supplements, no interactions.

And it should have been okay when I gave it to her, except for one thing. High doses of zinc can increase someone's risk for kidney stones, especially if you have existing kidney stones. One more time, keep this in mind for later.

Was that a kitchen remodel I mentioned earlier? Yes, a kitchen remodel! Right smack in the middle of the chaos toward the middle/end of my pregnancy, and the kicker? Manny was going to do it all on his own. He planned to gut the kitchen and tear down the walls between the kitchen/dining room/living room to have one big open room. Because why not?

The open concept was my idea, because I wanted to be able to see Ava from anywhere I was, for her safety. With two little babies coming, I wouldn't have the luxury of sitting or staying near Ava to keep my eyes on her. So, the walls had to come down.

When we bought our house, it needed a lot of cosmetic help. The kitchen was the last of the inside face lift, and I couldn't wait for it to be done. It was ugly AF, straight out of the seventies. We refinanced our mortgage and took cash out to help cover the cost of our remodel. That was in April, 2011. We were so excited and ended up booking our dumpster to arrive June 1, so we could get this kitchen *done*.

Also on June 1, I had a very special appointment planned, with a perinatal specialist, to be sure all was good with the pregnancy. I trusted my Ob-Gyn, but I needed reassurance from someone who sees high-risk pregnancies all the time, in order for me to believe it. I had to make sure all my T's were crossed and my I's were dotted.

Ava had acted weird the night before that appointment, like she was uncomfortable. She has major issues with constipation, so I thought maybe she was extra backed-up. I'd planned on dealing with that later on in the day, doing an extra suppository session with her. The morning of my appointment, she threw up. Again, I thought it was probably just constipation, since she hadn't been anywhere to pick up a virus.

I kept telling myself all this because I *had* to go to that appointment. I'd booked it months ago. Up to this point, there'd been no way I could leave Ava when she wasn't well: I was always there for her. This time, I had to push that fear aside and put the twins' health and my health ahead of hers. I had horrible guilt, though, because I felt, whichever choice I made, one of my children could potentially suffer from it.

The appointment was only fifteen minutes away, and while I was in the doctor's office, Manny called me twice to tell me Ava had thrown up several more times. Again, I thought, *really*? I can't even get through an appointment for *me* without friggin' chaos? *UGH*. There wasn't anything I could do about it, so I told him to only call if there was an emergency and to let me finish my appointment.

The specialist was wonderful. He praised me over and over again. It's not something I was used to hearing, because Manny and I just do what we need to do, not for praise. But hearing this man who specializes in high-risk pregnancies tell me I was an amazingly strong woman and praise me for taking such good care of myself while also being caregiver for Ava… Man, I needed to hear all that. I felt so seen and appreciated. It was so nice to have someone notice my extra effort and hard work and call me out on it. I honestly didn't want to leave. But I had to. Ava needed me.

The appointment itself went perfectly, something I hadn't experienced in forever. He told me the twins looked great, he had no concerns about them, and he had no concerns about me. He wasn't worried about me needing bed rest, and since I had been lifting Ava all along, I could continue to do so until it was too uncomfortable for me. Could not have been a better appointment. Thank God!

When I got home, Ava continued to throw up. I had been hoping she'd stop or slow down, because that dumpster we ordered? It was on its way that afternoon. Also on its way was a *huge* severe thunderstorm. High winds, excessive lightning, some hail. But not only did Ava not slow down, she was throwing up more and seemed like she was in pain. We couldn't wait for the dumpster. We had to get her to the ER. We had just gotten inside the ER when the storm hit *and,* back at home, the dumpster was delivered.

At the ER, I met God. Not the God you are thinking of. No, this was a man. A doctor. The most arrogant, male-chauvinistic human with a God complex I had ever met in my life. When he asked why we were there, I filled him in on all of the details, plus a little of Ava's history with vomiting, malrotation, etc. For some reason, my brain is able to hold every single detail about Ava, so I am the one that does the talking.

The whole time I spoke, he *never* looked at me. He looked at Manny. He asked Manny questions. I would answer. He belittled the fact that I was concerned about her vomiting and said I was just overreacting because I was pregnant, that she just had a virus. There was a lot more, but I'd rather not revisit that. He was *such an asshole.*

I think fire shot out of my eyes. It took everything in me to not totally lose it on him. I am a pretty easygoing person usually, but I do have an Irish temper if pushed just a little too much. Oh yeah, and I had pregnancy hormones that intensified my rage. But I was able to handle it with grace and stay off of the evening news that night.

I decided I was done with him and wanted her admitted. It turns out, that was a great decision. She was admitted in the early morning hours of June 2, and we didn't go back home until the June 23. It was *not* just a virus. I *wasn't* overreacting because I was pregnant. I was simply advocating for my daughter because she couldn't talk, and I was making sure she got the proper care she needed and deserved. Take that, you asshat.

That was one of the first moments when I realized my gut wasn't based on drama—it was fact. This was me mothering with my instincts first and their credentials second. I often say I have a PhD in Ava that far surpasses anything taught in medical books.

The attending physician told me she had pancreatitis. Didn't make sense to me. I saw her labs were off, so that's what should have been going on, but I just didn't "feel" it was the proper diagnosis. I had such a strong feeling about that. But I was still kind of new at this hospital stuff, so I didn't push too much. I let them treat her, and when things weren't going how they should, like not improving at all, my gut instincts began to make more sense.

The hospital wasn't really looking for any other diagnosis, so I took it upon myself to call her gastroenterologist specialist privately. I asked her, if something was wrong somewhere else in Ava's gut (like with the malrotation or something else), could it affect the lipase levels and make it *seem* like she had pancreatitis, when she really didn't?

She said yes, but she couldn't say anything more because Ava was not currently in her care. She told me that your whole gut can be thrown off from one organ being affected. And, well, Ava is different, so anything is possible. Unless Ava was at their hospital and under her care, though, she couldn't really say more. I respected that. I was frustrated but had to accept it.

I took what she said and tried to look into it more. Google wasn't what it is today, so my research didn't get me anywhere. But almost two weeks into our stay, they took a urine sample. When I saw the nurse hold up the cup, I couldn't believe what I saw. It looked like a snow globe. Like she had just shaken a snow globe.

I questioned what it was, and she shrugged it off, saying she'd never seen urine like that before, but the lab would tell us. The lab never did say anything, even though I was very vocal about my concern to the nurse, the nurse's desk, the doctor, and the lab. I knew it meant something. But what? Now I'd never know. Ugh.

During this hospital stay, one of my friends hosted a baby shower for me at her home, for which I was so extremely grateful. She was a twin mom herself, so I had already been asking her a bazillion questions about all things twins. She also helped me make my registry list and gave me been there/done that advice for what worked and what didn't. Man, was she a godsend for me!

I had Manny bring me a dress I could throw on at the hospital and wear to the shower. After the baby shower, I loaded all of the stuff into our minivan and headed back to the hospital. Manny had to go home and bring all the gifts inside himself, where they all sat until Ava and I got home later that month.

Insert pity party for me here. Again, another thing that wasn't "normal" for me. I wasn't able to enjoy the shower in the moment, because I was forty-five minutes away from my little soul mate in the hospital. I was worried about her, I was tired, I was anxious, and I was in total survival mode. I tried my absolute best to put on a brave face, but I was falling apart inside. I've always carried a little guilt from that day. My friends went out of their way to help me feel special, and I wasn't able to show them the utter gratitude I felt for them, for doing that. I will never forget that kindness.

It felt as if there were two versions of me existing at the same time: the smiling, grateful, pregnant-with-twins mom opening gifts, and the hospital mom whose heart never left Ava's bedside. In moments like that, I didn't know how to ask Manny—or anyone else, really—for the kind of emotional support I really needed. It was easier to just muscle through and pretend I was fine. No one could truly understand what it felt like to be me.

Back at the hospital afterward, I changed a bit. Somewhere during that time, I stopped feeling like "just" a mom and started stepping into the role of her full-time case manager, advocate, and translator—roles no one trains you for, but you take on because there's no other option.

I came to the realization that this hospital stay so far wasn't getting anywhere. I was not confident at all about how they were caring for Ava. For starters, I had to keep fighting with them to increase her fluids in her IV, because she had a kidney stone. I mean, was it really such a bother to up her fluids? They had her on maintenance fluids, and I knew she was already so far behind on her daily fluid intake.

Then came the whole urine sludge issue–the snow globe stuff in the urine sample. That was it for me. I just knew that meant something and all parties involved had failed Ava. I ended up asking if she could get transferred up to the bigger hospital, where they knew her. This was back when the two hospitals not only didn't converse with each other, they actually kind of had beef with each other. So, it was not easy to get the doctors locally to talk to her specialists up north.

We did end up being transferred, which meant we were even farther away from home. The dumpster had been sitting in our front yard for two weeks now, empty, while we continued to pay for it. When we went to the hospital farther away, Manny went to work during the day and came up to see us every other night. Life was going on while we were stuck in the hospital. Trees were budding, things were turning green, and, oh yeah, my prenatal appointments were getting missed.

It took almost two more weeks before we were able to get home after that transfer and stay at our vacation home up north. Seems like it should be called that, for the number of long weekends and weeks we'd spent there. They, unlike the other hospital, listened to me and investigated a bit more to find out what was happening.

Turns out, when Ava was vomiting, it wasn't a virus. It also wasn't pancreatitis. She was *full* of kidney stones. That sludge I saw in the urine that looked like a snow globe? Kidney stones. It was sediment, like sand, that she'd passed into her urine. So, that discomfort I saw the night before she got admitted? She was trying to pass the stones that then broke up into sediment.

My brain went into overload. Just because I now knew what the cause was for her stay, I wasn't satisfied. I needed to know *WHY* this had happened and how to make damn sure it never happened again.

Why did Ava go from having just one kidney stone that had been stable for years to being full of stones? What happens now to all of the stones that are still in her kidneys? Will she have to pass them herself? Would she need them surgically removed?

This was where the perfect storm came into play. It started with putting her feet in casts, then the stomach bug. What completed the hat trick and caused the perfect storm was the high dose supplementation of zinc. All three can cause kidney stones for a normal, healthy person. But for a child like Ava, who is severely physically impaired, it's a higher risk. Combine all three along with not hydrating her properly over a span of under six months, and we had the epitome of a perfect storm.

Once I connected those dots, I stopped seeing our individual medical events as random bad luck and started to see how every decision, every "it's no big deal," could potentially stack together. It made me a better advocate, a more educated mom, and, if I'm honest, a more concerned one, too. The most heartbreaking part of all of this was the things that got Ava into this predicament were painful, and now it would be even more painful for her to get out of it. She was going to have to physically pass all of this sediment and the piles of stones that filled her kidneys.

There were a few big stones she would not be able to pass on her own; she would end up needing to have emergency surgery to remove those. Since she was nonverbal, I asked how I'd know if one was stuck. I was told, "Oh, you will know," when that level of pain was reached and to bring her to the ER. There was nothing I could do to help her, and there was no way I could explain to her what had to happen.

There I was, almost thirty weeks pregnant and at the point in my pregnancy when I had to go in to the doctors twice a week—one day for a stress test and ultrasound, and another day for a doctor's appointment, always with Ava in tow. I also had to go through all of those gifts from my baby shower, which had been weeks earlier and were still just sitting in our house.

I needed to wash all the new baby clothes, bibs, etc., write thank you cards, put together furniture, and get things ready for the twins. On top of all of that, I still had to be Ava's full-time caregiver, which included her tube feeds, meds, therapy appointments, doctor appointments, and suppository sessions, watching for seizures, and now, watching for and collecting kidney stones... Overwhelmed is an understatement for how I felt.

I was living in this strange split world where one part of me was nesting for and getting excited for two new babies and the other part was bracing for the next medical crisis with my first child.

God definitely looked out for us during the next few months—this time, the real Big Guy, not the asshole ER doctor. We made it through the birth of the twins and brought in the New Year without any more trouble from little Miss Ava. She stayed out of the hospital, remained healthy, and didn't have any issues with the kidney stones.

Also, during that time, I got to know Ava's new nephrologist very well, along with his nurse. To this day, he is one of my absolute favorite of Ava's specialists. He was the most thorough, intelligent, yet personable and caring doctor and human I've met. His nurse was equally as incredible, and Ava and I grew quite fond of both of them immediately. I am so thankful that these two are the medical professionals who helped Ava through the next decade of absolute hell with these kidney stones. Yes, *decade*.

In reality, it was more than a decade. While I've mentioned on social media that Ava has struggled with kidney stones over the years, I've never truly shared what it was like, going through it. Mostly because I didn't want to sound like a complainer, but also because I didn't think people really wanted to know what was going on. I didn't want to be known as "that person." You know, the one who complains about everything, so everyone can see they just want attention. Attention was definitely not something I was looking for, so when anyone asked how Ava was doing, I just spit out facts like, "passed another stone," or "she's stable." I never went into what it was like for us to experience that decade of those little bitches, aka her kidney stones.

From a social media perspective or to anyone I was around in person, Ava and I were happily living our lives. Online or in person, I looked like the mom who had figured it out. But offline and in private, I was the mom who cried in hospital bathrooms and in the car before walking into Target.

One of the concerns (well *fears)* I had about having another baby was what would I do if Ava had to go into the hospital while we had another child to care for? Who would watch that child while Manny went to work? We didn't need to worry about that when it was just the three of us, but now we were a party of five. Once again, I was about to face that fear head on and find out what we would do.

Shortly after the New Year, in February 2012, when the twins were six months old, Ava was showing some very intense pain. I knew it was another stone or sediment she was working on, because of how she acted. She grimaced and made little growls once in a while, pulling her feet up to her face. She pulled her legs in against herself very hard, trying to find some relief. If she happened to be in her wheelchair or on her stander when the kidney stone pain hit, she would make what I call upside-down hands. She'd bring them to her face, upside-down, and shake them. But the one thing she always did, no matter what position, was turn her top lip under. It became known as the "kidney lip."

If Ava was acting uncomfortable or looked like maybe she didn't feel good and I saw the kidney lip, it was just a kidney stone passing. I didn't have to evaluate her any further. If I didn't see a kidney lip, then I had to take her temperature, check her ears, scan her body, looking for any signs of pain or discomfort, and watch for clues to determine what was wrong. In that way, knowing it was "just a kidney stone" was easy.

That day in February, her pain appeared to be much more intense than usual. It sounds crazy to say *more* intense, because *any* kidney stone is one of the most intense pains a human can face. I've been told by ER doctors that 2mm stones can make the biggest, strongest, toughest dude drop to his knees and yell in pain with a tear in his eye. I actually had the pleasure of experiencing kidney stones myself when I was pregnant with Ava, so I know from personal experience just how intense the pain is. So, for me to notice out of the gate that she was experiencing more pain, I knew it couldn't be good.

Ava's pain usually came and went when she was passing smaller stones or sediment. And when I say smaller stones, I mean stones ranging from beach sand size up to 3mm or 4mm. No joke—Ava is a total badass. She has passed up to a 6mm stone on her own at home! The pain would come in waves: when the stone moved, she'd show all signs of pain; and when it stopped, she went back to her happy, lovable self. Like a switch would turn off and on. When it was on, it was *ON*. When it was off, it was like it had never happened. Man, is she a person to strive to be like or what? She would just move on and not dwell on it any longer than she had to. She ended up being my greatest teacher without ever speaking a word…

When this extra pain arose, I had a discussion with the nephrologist and the urologist, and they had us get imaging then told us to head up north to the hospital. It turned out she had a stuck stone and needed emergency surgery to have it removed. That meant we'd be in the hospital for at least two days. But with Ava's track record, that meant most likely three to four days.

Well, shit. What the F do we do now? What would we do with the twins? I mean, they had to eat, have bottles, and baths, and they needed diapers and wipes, clothes, and toys. OMG. My head was spinning. Where would they stay? How would Manny work?

My fear of trying to juggle it all was coming to life. I needed my mother so badly in that moment. She would know what to do. But me? I was trying to balance it all—being there for Ava while also worrying about her and her surgery; worrying about how Manny could work, because if he doesn't work, he doesn't get paid; and worrying about how we would still be able to give the twins what they needed, plus also physically care for them and where.

Manny and I were both drowning in our own concerns, but instead of leaning on each other, it often felt like we were each just grabbing a different corner of the crisis and hoping it wouldn't collapse.

Manny suggested they could stay at a hotel down the street from the hospital. While there is a home offered to families by the hospital, where they can stay when their kiddos are inpatient, we had never taken advantage of it. We both just hadn't felt comfortable doing that, because there are families that truly need to stay there. We had the means to stay at a private hotel, so that is what happened, leaving the other rooms open for families who didn't have that option.

The surgery was successful in that they were able to break up the stuck stone. The urologist told us it was a 7mm stone, too big to pass on its own, that got lodged in Ava's ureter. He was able to blast it but was unable to remove the blasted fragments, which meant they were added to the smaller full stones and sediment already in there. Unfortunately for Ava, she would still have to pass the broken pieces, on top of everything else.

Once again, Ava didn't have a clean solution. Once again, she had to continue dealing with something for much longer than anyone else. Once again, we took one step forward and ten steps back. As I'd grown accustomed to, rather than working through what was happening to me internally during yet another traumatic event, I just filed it away.

Nothing seemed to work in Ava's favor, and if I got upset about each one, I'd end up being upset all the time. So, I began to master my coping mechanism of just saying, "It is what it is," pushing down inside me my feelings and reactions, my sadness or fear or anger or disappointment, so I could deal with the situation happening right in front of me.

At this point in my journey as Ava's mother, I realized the "light at the end of the tunnel" I had always focused on was starting to dim. It was becoming harder and harder to think we'd ever be able to exhale. That we'd ever be able to just "live" without a fear of seizures, fear of another malrotation, or now a fear of kidney stones getting stuck or a horrible kidney infection, on top of just struggling with Ava requiring constant tube feeds, diaper changes, and handicap accessibility for her entire life. She was not only not overcoming any of her issues, she was accumulating more and more the older she got.

I felt defeated, beat up, and pretty emotional after hearing from the urologist, but Ava was not having that. She said, "Not on my watch bitch—ha-ha." That night in the hospital, she decided to have a 2:00 a.m. desaturation episode that required a code to be called, "Respiratory to room xxxx stat," on the intercom. And instantly, all of my self-pitying feeling and "oh, poor me" mentality about my future being so hard as her mother, disappeared. Seeing all those people come running to Ava's bedside snapped me back to reality. All I wanted was her to be alive in that moment. Nothing else mattered.

They aren't sure what happened or why, but they were able to stabilize her. Then, they all went back to their stations. But me? *Me*? I had had a whole new fear unlocked. I wondered, what the F just happened? And if they didn't know why it happened, will it happen again?

There was no way I was going to be able to sleep at all after that, and I also knew there was no way I could do this alone anymore. I called Manny and told him, once the twins got up and ate, they needed to come to the hospital.

Ava never did crash again, but she was slow to recover, which is typical for Ava. They had to be sure she was out of the clear for respiratory issues and for infection, so we ended up needing a few more days in the hospital. But here's the thing… I told Manny he was not leaving me alone. I couldn't handle that code again. Normally, that would be okay, but we had two babies who needed somewhere to go.

What did we do? We had them sleep in their car seats on the opposite side of Ava's bed, where no one could see them. Ava got the comfy bed, but Manny and me? We slept in chairs that didn't even recline. The whole Laurencio party of five spent those days in the hospital as one unit.

We did it, though. We actually made it through one of situations I'd feared would happen. It wasn't perfect, but the twins were fed, they got to see their mama, and I got to see them. We all adapted to the situation. I truly think, having them there, allowed me to focus on some normalcy, helped me from crashing during that stay. It turned out having them nearby while dealing with a medical situation with Ava was more healing for me than stressful. It could not have gone better, if you ask me.

Even though we got through and went home, Ava still had many, many years of pain to follow, over ten more years of it. There just aren't words to explain my full sense of dread for what was to come. After knowing how excruciating the pain in passing a stone, knowing I had to just watch her go through it and not be able to do anything, knowing she had years more of this in her future and I was not able to explain any of it to her—that is a mental and emotional suffering and dread I wish upon no one. It is such a feeling of absolute helplessness.

Also being a stay-at-home mom to my healthy, active little twinnies was a lot to endure. They were doing all they were supposed to—crawling, getting into everything, and wanting my attention all day long. It was such a beautiful time for me, being able to witness and experience the joy of my children hitting their milestones and interacting with each other, doing all the things that typical, developing children do. But it was an equally dark time, having to watch Ava suffer through so much pain with her kidney stones and to also watch her falling behind in development compared to her infant siblings.

It was such a very emotional, stressful, heartbreaking, exhausting, *and* beautiful time, all wrapped in one. I felt like two different mothers sharing one body—the mom who was cheering on first steps, and the mom quietly grieving the steps that might never come for Ava.

While my sweet Ava was already dealing with one of the three most excruciatingly painful medical conditions a person could endure, another, far worse medical condition was waiting just around the corner.

Pancreatitis.

Pancreatitis

Nothing prepares you for the moment when your child starts fighting for her life.
And the woman who emerges afterward is not the one who walked in.

2015 started out as a pretty awesome year. One of the best years in a very long time.

At the beginning of January, Ava had been out of school for quite a while because she had no nursing coverage. She requires one-on-one support for everything, and with her epilepsy and tube feeds, she requires an RN to accompany her at school and on the bus ride. The RN needs to be able to administer medications, her tube feeds, and treat the accompanying medical issues that go along with her epilepsy.

While the school can assign a nurse for her, I had declined their offer. I didn't want someone I didn't know and hadn't ever met assigned to Ava. It had to be someone I liked and was comfortable with, plus was a good fit for the entire family.

It also had to be someone who had spent a good amount of time with Ava in order to understand and learn all about her mannerisms, her personality, and the way she communicates without words. But most importantly, it had to be someone I could trust 100% to be the caregiver for my Ava.

I had been working through a local nursing agency for over a year, trying to find an RN who could not only take Ava to school, but could also provide coverage outside of school, in our home. Having a nurse in the home is something I have fought having from day one, but man, did I need some help.

I have always been the type of person who, if I can do something myself, I just do it. I don't ask for help or delegate tasks, unless it is something just not possible for me to handle. But I felt my stress building as the years went on, and added to that fact was the twins were going to be starting preschool in the fall, so I desperately needed extra hands. Not gonna lie, it would also be nice to have a grownup adult to talk to during the day, instead of either non-verbal Ava or two crazy toddlers—ha-ha.

As you can imagine, it's a lot of work just to get twins ready and out the door to go anywhere or do anything, but add to that Ava, with her wheelchair, and it's a whole other level. If we need to be somewhere during a meal time, I also need to bring all of Ava's feeding supplies—feeding pump, feed bag, syringes, water for flushes, food, etc. I also need to bring her seizure meds, diapers, wipes, change of clothes (just in case), and an EpiPen for Jillian, because of her peanut allergy and an epi pen for Desmond for his coconut allergy.

With their allergies, we couldn't just get food when we were out, so I usually needed to bring food/snacks for the twins, too. Much easier to keep them safe from potential exposure or cross-contamination. Years of doing this all by myself was really starting to take its toll on me, and I finally gave in and asked for help.

I found our nurse, Marjie, through word of mouth. At Ava's annual IEP meeting, the IEP team had asked how it was going on my search for a nurse for her, so they could estimate when she'd return to school. I told them I wasn't really getting anywhere with the nursing agency. I was actually trying through two different agencies with zero luck.

One of the women in the meeting spoke up and said she'd heard of a nurse who was looking for a child to accompany at this school. She had been a nurse for another child who had gone to the school previously but that child had since passed away. After a bit of time off, she'd decided she wanted to come back, because she loved doing what she did. I agreed to meet her.

From the moment I met Marjie, I just knew she was the one, our forever nurse. I feel like she was given to us as a gift from God. Sounds so dramatic, but I am dead serious. She was a perfect fit for our family in so many ways. Besides her incredible experience from her nursing career and experience in her own personal life, raising a child of her own with medical challenges, she just seemed to become part of our family seamlessly. I have always felt weird, calling her Ava's nurse, because she became more like a second mother to me, grandmother to my children, and honestly, one of the best friends I have ever had in my life.

I trusted her 100%, and for the first time in Ava's and the twins' lives, I started to be able to go and do things on my own. For example, I was able to leave Ava in her care and not have to worry one bit. Manny and I were able to go on some dinner dates, some lunch dates, and to some parties that my friends hosted. We even got to take the twins to the beach! That was super-duper huge for me to be able to do, because up until that point, I could not leave the house if Manny wasn't home.

When the twins started preschool in early fall of that year, I am not sure if I was more excited than they were. Things were beginning to feel "normal" with this newfound freedom I had, because of Marjie. The twins being able to participate in something outside of the home was another thing I had been dreaming of. It was incredible to watch them experience something on their own, not as Ava's siblings, but as individuals. To be around other kids their own age and start to develop their own little friends and personalities.

I drove them to school in the morning, and after dropping them off, I'd get a coffee and do a little shopping at TJ Maxx or Target in those few hours I had to myself. This may sound so minor to someone, but being able to do that just two days a week was something I never thought would happen for me. I had been trapped in my home up until that point, with my days and nights revolving around my children for all of their lives. So, to be able to go to Target and browse around like the other moms felt like winning the lottery.

You know that feeling when you have a newborn and you just can't wait for things to slow down? How you can't wait until the feedings are spaced more apart and your baby sleeps longer, so you can have some time back to yourself? Or for a time when the diaper changes and bottles give you a little more breathing room in between feeds? Well, my life after having Ava up until that moment had felt like a never-ending newborn stage. So, just as a new mother is absolutely thrilled to browse around Target among the other adults, I was equally happy. Even though my "baby" was twelve years old at the time.

One of the best days of my life was October 31, 2015. The twins were taking part in a Halloween concert at their preschool, and they were *so* excited. I was pretty excited, too. Desmond was a baby spider, and Jillian was Cinderella, of course. Desmond told me he had to be a baby spider—he could not be a regular spider. I have no idea how I found an actual baby spider costume for him, but I did. They both begged to wear their costumes every day before the concert, but had to wait until Halloween. They were busting at the seams to finally put on their costumes and perform for the parents at their preschool.

I loved every minute of it.

This concert, this moment, is exactly what I had dreamed of from the time I got pregnant with Ava. I had been to so many performances, sports games, graduations, birthday parties, etc., for my nieces and nephews over the past decades, and now, it was finally *my* kid who was performing. What a feeling.

I will never forget sitting in the audience with a smile on my face so big, my cheeks hurt. I looked around at the other parents and just felt such an immense sense of not just pride, but belonging. I, me, Lisa Laurencio, had children who were able not only to walk, talk and eat on their own, but who were able to be part of a performance! That was something I had never had a chance to experience before, and I will never, ever forget it.

The performance was even better than I could have imagined. Desmond was just a doll, but he was actually super-shy. I don't think he took his eyes off of me the whole time! Jillian, on the other hand, definitely made up for his shyness... She completely led the show. She sang the loudest, and she made sure to tell the whole audience that her friend's costume was pretty and that they should tell her so. She was a complete ham. She had the parents in stitches; everyone was laughing at her, at *my* child. Not because of her disability, but for her personality. Man, life was freaking good that day.

I recorded the whole performance on my phone, and I could not wait to get home and edit some of it to post on social media. It would have been the first time I could brag on *my* kids for something they were part of! Pinch me! This has to be a dream.

When we got home from the school, Marjie told us that Ava had been showing signs of discomfort while we were gone. We all assumed it was another kidney stone, since she still had a lot of stones left to pass. She had been up a few nights before with some intense pain, so it wasn't a shock to see her in pain again. She still hadn't passed anything from that night, so we'd just assumed it was most likely the stone had started moving again. Soon, we'd see her hard work appear in her diaper.

Except the pain didn't stop. Not only did it not stop, she was becoming more uncomfortable. I'd never seen her show this level of discomfort. Then, she started vomiting. Fear instantly consumed me, because I felt as if I'd been transported back in time to her malrotation. They said there was a chance of it happening again and to be on the lookout for any signs of it. This was more than a sign. I felt she was in danger. *I knew she was in danger.*

Because of the potentially grave situation and the rate at which she seemed to be declining, we called an ambulance.

We knew how quickly things could turn for her, and having her sit in the waiting room in the ER on Halloween night, a Friday night, was not a chance I wanted to take. So, 911 it was.

As you can imagine, the entire emergency room was packed. Ava and I got thrown in a room in the back and were told that the doctor would be in shortly. It was just us girls, because Manny had to stay home with the twins. When I peeked outside of the room, I saw a man covered head to toe in blood, lying on a cot in the hallway just outside our door. The entire ER was packed, with cots full of bodies lining the hallway. There were people moaning and yelling, plus lots of frantic hospital workers scattering about. It felt like I was in a movie. The ER is not the place you want to be on Halloween night.

Shortly after we got there, Ava started to throw up green. Being the researcher I am, I already knew that green vomit could be a sign of malrotation, and if that happens, surgery is required ASAP or the intestines can die, and so can the patient.

I rang the nurse's bell, and when she came in, she assured me the doctor was on his way. I was very understanding of the situation and didn't get angry with her, but I tried to explain that she could literally die if not treated in time.

"I think she needs to be bumped up on the list to be seen," I told her.

Right after I said those words, I started to cry. I'd never lost my composure during any of Ava's previous medical events, so I was so surprised when it happened. I tried to explain to the nurse that I'm never emotional during any of

Ava's medical stuff and the fact that I was now meant something. My body knew Ava was in danger.

She probably just thought I was a regular mom, freaking out because their child was sick. She had no idea who I truly was. How could she?

She simply apologized that we had to wait due to the packed ER and said she would see what she could do to get the doctor in as soon as he was done with his current patient. Then, she left.

After the nurse left, something happened that had never happened before and hasn't happened since. Ava screamed. I didn't know she *could* scream. With all of her kidney stones, even with the 7mm stone that got stuck, the most she had ever done was growl.

This time, though, she let out a loud, horrifying, blood-curdling scream. When I heard it, it felt like everything else in the ER fell silent. All I could hear was her. Every nerve in my body felt it, every hair stood up. She only screamed once, and while it was not long at all, it felt like time stood still. A shiver went down my spine. I immediately scooped her up in my arms and went into the hall, which still looked like a scene from *The Walking Dead,* shouting that I needed someone in here *NOW*!

I can only imagine what we looked like, standing there: me with my eyes filled with terror, holding Ava's totally limp, pale body in my arms.

For the first time, I completely lost it. I was sobbing uncontrollably when the nurse came. I tried to explain the meaning of Ava's scream and that I just knew something was incredibly wrong and that she was dying. Right at that moment, the doctor rushed in and told me that we were going to get transferred to the hospital up north to the ICU stat. He told me she was indeed a very sick little girl and needed care that they could not provide.

He told me that she had pancreatitis.

Pancreatitis? *What*? That's what they'd told me a few years prior to this, when in fact she was just full of kidney stones. So, I thought, here we go again. No, that can't be it. He assured me that, without a doubt, she did indeed have pancreatitis, and then he told me that her lipase level was the highest he had ever seen: 4,444. The normal range is between 0 and 60. I'm sorry, *WHAT*?!

Even hardcore alcoholics don't get levels that high. So how could a twelve-year-old child who was tube fed with a controlled diet and who had never touched a drop of alcohol in her life not only get pancreatitis, but such a severe, acute form of it? My brain immediately wanted to whip out my laptop, start researching, and get to the bottom cause of it, but there wasn't time. Ava was fighting for her life, and I needed to keep my full attention on her.

I knew this wasn't just another medical hurdle for her.

No, this was going to be a battle for her life.

I did not sleep a single second for the next two and a half days. I couldn't. I was her voice, as I was the only one who knew her and the only one there with her. I was the one who had been through every single moment in Ava's life. I had to stay awake. I had to help them figure her out, to be available to answer any and all questions.

I had to be the one to process it all and be able to ask all the right questions, based on her medical history, which I had completely stored in my brain. I had to be the one to approve certain care, tests, and procedures. There was a constant flow of people in and out of her room in the ICU, day and night. They needed the information I had, and she needed me to be able to stay awake to fight for her. Sleep felt selfish, not required.

She was intubated and put into a medically induced coma. She stayed like that for what seemed like forever, but really was for just under a week. I did eventually go to sleep, only because I was forced to. The nurses made me try to sleep. Even with that, I couldn't sleep more than an hour at a time, because I had to get up and check on her.

I also had to keep letting Manny know what was going on, because he was helplessly stuck at home with the twins. Unless I updated him, he had no idea what was going on. I'm glad we are made differently, because there is no way I could have been able to be an hour and a half away from Ava while trying to keep a sense of normalcy at home for the twins. Huge kudos to him for that superpower.

Manny is a self-employed plumber. He works for himself, by himself. He has no employees, and he likes it that way—ha-ha. So, when I say things like, if he doesn't work, he doesn't get paid, it's our reality. There is no one who can continue the work or jobs he has going on, so it just stops. Because of that, he needs to work, regardless of what is going on in our lives, because, unfortunately, the mortgage, the health insurance premium, and all the monthly bills—they still keep coming. He has no paid sick days and no paid vacations. No work = no income.

And, as luck would have it (I say that in the most sarcastic tone), he had just started a massive job for a bus depot. It was originally supposed to be him and an employee he had when he signed the contract, but things didn't work out with that employee, so Manny had been left to do it solo. It was a big job for even two people, but now, it was even more so, because he had no extra help. He *had* to go to this job, and he *had* to work long days to make up for the one-man show. The timing could not have been worse. Just our Laurencio luck.

This was where Marjie truly showed us just how incredibly amazing and selfless she is. Without a second thought, she stepped in and took on the full responsibility of the twins' care, lifting it from Manny and letting them stay at her house during the weekdays. Manny would drop them off on Sunday night, work as long as he needed to each day during the week, then pick them up after work on Friday night. He was living the life of a single dad—ha-ha.

It truly couldn't have worked out more perfectly for us, because the stress of the twins being safe and well cared for was gone. While I was bummed that we had to pull them out of the preschool they loved, Marjie was the next best thing. She kept them fed and bathed them, washed their clothes, and put them to bed—she did it all. She kept them busy during the day, doing crafts, baking, and taking them to the park, the library, and out with her family for dinner. She even had them help collect her chickens' eggs. That allowed me to exhale a little bit and focus on being present for Ava, while Manny was able to focus on his work, knowing that the twins were living their best life at Marjie's house. They really were living their best life. Shit, I'd have loved to have been in their shoes and stayed with Marjie!

While Manny had such a stressful time, balancing work at such a demanding job on a time constraint while also being away from Ava, plus bringing me clothes and visiting/sleeping over at the hospital twice a week, and then doing the full-time dad gig on the weekends, I envied him. He got to drive to work every day, sleep comfortably in our bed all alone each night, and just have fun with the twins on the weekends. At least, that is how I saw it.

Even if I "could" have left the hospital to work or be home with the twins, I wouldn't have. I struggled just to leave the room long enough to use the bathroom, so leaving the hospital was never going to happen. Yet, I envied him. I was jealous about how his regular life still continued. Sure, he was stressed. And yes, it was also his child in the ICU, too. But even with that, he still got to go to work like he would have if Ava was at home and he got to spend time with the twins on the weekends, just as he would, if Ava was home. And for those reasons, I was jealous.

He got to sleep in our bed all alone every night–our typical sleeping arrangements include me, him, and Ava sleeping together in the bed, for her safety. He could come home from work each day to a quiet house, no wild twins to care for or wrangle. He could go to bed when he wanted, watch what he wanted on TV, and eat what he wanted. He was living the life of a bachelor—ha-ha.

I couldn't help but think, from my point of view, that not only was his life continuing "as is," with him still working during the week and spending time with the twins on the weekends, but he got a lot of time alone. All while I was living in complete and total hell, surrounded by the constant sound of beeping, sleeping in a pull-out chair, and feeling like I'd abandoned our twins and missing them terribly, all while watching Ava go through so much.

While I was very grateful when he made the drive up to the hospital two times a week, it also hurt. He always arrived so exhausted, then would sit with Ava while I "put away" the clothes he'd brought for me and pack up the dirties for him to take home. He then would leave to go grab food from the cafeteria, eat, and, with the full belly, just go to sleep.

He never really "visited" me. Not once would he ask how I was, only about how Ava was doing. Not how I was holding up, not how I was coping, not if I was scared, lonely, or traumatized. He wasn't trying to be malicious. He truly didn't see it. But that's exactly what hurt—I felt like no one saw it. Like no one saw me.

He showed up physically. But emotionally, I felt like I was in that hospital completely alone.

I felt like it was always me who had to give up everything. I used to work full time before having Ava. I was the one who carried the health insurance before having Ava. I had a good job in the finance department, working from home, before having Ava. I gave that up, became a mom and full-time caregiver, then was thrown into raising twins and Ava, while he got to return to work when the babies were just a week and a half old. It didn't seem fair. While I didn't want to leave, I was starting to feel bitter that I *couldn't* leave. It was almost like it was just expected of me now.

I hated what I was going through. Wasn't all of the bullshit Ava and I had already gone through enough? Why was it me who always had to sacrifice, had to adjust, had to adapt? I'd lost every single part of what made me *me.* At this point, I felt so incredibly alone, and I had no one to talk to about it. Man, did I ever need my mom at that time. Just a quick hug or shoulder to cry on.

I wasn't sure if I was feeling this way because I was extremely sleep-deprived, had been through some pretty traumatic things in the past week, or was already feeling stir crazy, being stuck in the hospital room, surrounded by a gazillion machines that beeped all day and night. This wasn't a typical thought pattern for me.

I mean, that *had* to be the reason. Things always seem so much worse when you are stressed. Being in the ICU with your child, sitting bedside 24/7 while she is intubated and not knowing what is going to happen is high-stress, right? I went with that thought and, once again, just pushed down the feelings. I didn't want to feel them, so I just decided not to feel them and sort of filed them away. I needed to be strong for Ava, and I couldn't let that way of thinking keep me from that.

During the next few weeks in the ICU, Ava continued to struggle quite a bit. She gained seventeen pounds in fluid just in one week! Not good. Her abdomen was so swollen. She ended up getting high fevers and a collapsed lung from the pressure of the swelling, which required an urgent chest tube. Not gonna lie, that was pretty awesome to watch. I had seen this kind of stuff on medical TV shows, but never in my reality.

I asked to suit up and stay in the room when they were going to place it, because I am a total medical nerd. They were like, um, okay… I think I might have been the first mom to ask. If they had asked me if I wanted to put in the chest tube myself, I would have said yes. That would have been awesome! Like, for real.

Ava also had to have a massive pancreatic cyst drained that was the size of a honeydew melon, along with its smaller sister. She was on TPN nutrition (being fed through a PICC line in her arm) and had a bazillion labs, X-rays, ultrasounds, and CT scans, plus what seemed like a procedure every other day.

Not to jump ahead, but she eventually had to have her gallbladder removed that following March from all of the inflammation and damage during the pancreatitis. When the surgeon removed it (the same surgeon who had repaired her malrotation), I once again heard, "We've never seen that before." He said that because her gallbladder literally fell apart in his hands. Damn.

I'll never forget, when we were about three weeks into our ICU stay in December, the GI said to me, "I am honestly surprised she didn't end up with multiple organ failure." Yeah, she was *that* sick.

Being in the ICU from Halloween to mid-December taught me a lot about myself, and I also developed new coping skills. First, I figured out, if I can't fix something or change something, I can at least make it funny. Second, no matter how hard I pray or how good a Christian I am, terrible things are going to happen to good people. That is fact.

When the doctors make their rounds in the ICU and you hear all of the scary things they are talking about, you can let yourself freak out or you can try to find the humor in the situation. There is always something to find to laugh about–hear me out.

For example, one morning, when the doctors were making their rounds, the lead doctor was talking about fentanyl for Ava and asked if I was okay with her being on it.

I said, "Sure! It's not like she's going to roll her wheelchair down the end of the driveway to make drug deals when we get home." What made it even funnier to me was how they all just stared at me when I said it—ha-ha!

Or when Ava's temperature was crazy high due to a bad infection, they kept a thermometer in her butt continuously. The nurse would come in to check the number, and I'd have them play "guess the temperature" game with me. I'd have everyone in the room take a guess just by touching her skin, and the closest one to the actual temperature would win. Of course, I won every time. Moms know best!

Growing up as a non-practicing Catholic, I thought that bad things just didn't happen to good people. I always thought, if I believed in God and basically did what was good in His eyes (for the most part, ha-ha), I'd be "rewarded" with my prayers being answered. Or that I'd be protected, like some invisible shield would not allow bad things to penetrate into my private little good-girl bubble.

Why was He not answering any of my prayers for Ava? I mean, even if, somehow, I didn't pass the "get into Heaven test," what was wrong with Ava? She is literally an angel here on Earth and does nothing but smile and bring joy to everyone who meets her. It made zero sense to me.

During that hospital stay, I lost my belief in Jesus and my complete faith that there is even a God at all. I started to think He really didn't exist and it didn't matter how good you were, no one was going to save you. There really isn't some "Guy in the Sky" who is going to somehow miraculously save my little girl. And that realization, that loss in my faith, was absolutely devastating.

It hardened my heart a bit.

It made me angry.

It made me feel like everything I had been taught was a lie.

Just during the time I spent in the ICU with Ava, a little under two months, I was exposed to things I never knew existed. Horrible things.

For one, I watched a beautiful, angelic one-year-old boy die as a result of his father's hand. Like I literally watched him, since he was in the room next to us. I saw it all. I even heard things the family talked about that I shouldn't have heard. I watched the incredibly loving nurses who had cared for him, gather the clothing for him to wear after he passed, for when the family came in to see him. I was in awe of their strength.

I watched special needs children get dumped into rooms all alone, no one staying with them, no one visiting them, left alone day and night, and probably frightened out of their minds, with no one to console or comfort them. They would arrive by ambulance alone or get transported from the group home they were living in.

I watched visitors show up drunk or on drugs to visit their kids. I watched a teenager fight for his life after getting hit by a train. In order for me to use the bathroom, I had to walk straight toward his room to get there. The bathroom was right next to his room, so I couldn't help but see him. Let's just say you don't want to see what someone looks like after they've been hit by a train.

So, if there is truly a God, why was this happening to these children? Why did He not hear my prayers that I personally prayed for that little boy? Why did He let him die due to the uncontrollable rage from his father? There had the be only one reason. Because, I decided, there isn't a God after all.

When we were finally transferred to the pediatrics floor shortly before Christmas, I should have been happy, but I was far from it.

When you are in the ICU, you have constant care. Someone is outside of your room when they aren't in the room, caring for you. Also, when you are one of the baddies, like Ava, you get a 1:1 nurse. In the pediatrics department, we went from constant attention and care, a revolving door of people in and out, to being put in a room at the far corner of the pediatrics floor, where we were left alone. Completely alone. I was lucky if someone came in every three to four hours. Ava no longer had constant monitoring, and even though it was safe for her and a welcome transition, this affected me a lot. I was not expecting to feel how I did. I felt almost depressed.

For the first time during the stay, I realized how truly alone I really was. I was updating Ava's status on my Facebook page, so no one really needed to call or text me to check on her. We were an hour and a half away from friends and family, so it was too far for most to come visit. So, while I wasn't upset that no one was calling or visiting, I started to feel hurt that no one did.

At the same time, I was so good at masking things—the close call to her having supper with Jesus, the daily stress of living in the hospital, the trauma we had been through and were still going through, the chronic stress from the accumulation of years of struggle, the guilt of leaving my twins, etc. Because of that, people probably thought I was fine. Plus, I had gotten so used to shutting people out, why would they visit or reach out to me?

In typical Lisa style, since there was nothing that I could do about it, I just pushed it down. I honestly couldn't deal with it at that time, because I was just trying to survive the days at that point. I also was trying to make sure the twins still had a Christmas. Just because Ava was in the hospital didn't mean that Santa would skip our house!

I made Christmas cards from photos I had already taken and had on my phone, ordered them, addressed them, and mailed them from the hospital. I ordered all of the gifts from Ava's bedside and had them shipped to the house.

I also decided that, this year, Christmas Day didn't have to fall on December 25, because, well, the twins didn't know what day that was. They were four years old, and we had pulled them out of preschool so they could stay at Marjie's during the day. They had no concept of how many days until Christmas, which took some of the stress away, but not of the pain.

We were able to bust out of the hospital just before Christmas. While Ava was still very sick, there really wasn't much I couldn't do at home to care for her on my own. That night, when I finally got home, I could not stop hugging my twins, just taking them in. My son was so damn cute that night. He was stuck to me like glue, following me everywhere, and whenever I sat down, he climbed up in my lap. I loved every single minute of it. I missed his snuggly little body way too much.

I will never forget one moment when he was sitting on my lap, facing away from me. I had my arms wrapped around him and was kissing his head as I said, "I promise I will never leave you again."

While I meant every word I said, I learned later that night I should never promise things that are not in my control…

That very night, at 3:00 a.m., I went back to the hospital to get Ava readmitted.

I know something changed in my son that day. I cannot imagine how his little heart shattered when he woke up and ran in to snuggle his mama, and she was gone. I mean, I'd promised him I would never leave him again. Not only did I break that promise, I didn't even stay home for twenty-four hours.

With all that I had been through up to that point, the feeling of deserting Desmond is one of the most heartbreaking things I experienced. I felt like what I'd done was unforgivable; it made me feel like such a horrible mother. I not only broke his heart that day, but I lost his trust, and that kills me.

Back at the hospital, Christmas decorations and festivities were well under way in the pediatrics unit. In all of the years I had stayed at the hospital with Ava, our "little girls only" getaways, as I liked to call them, we had yet to be inpatient during Christmas. We'd just stayed for our first Halloween and Thanksgiving, so it looked like she was going for the hat trick this time. Christmas in the hospital is not something I ever want to experience again.

The staff was more than incredible. They went over and above for the children. They allowed the parents to "shop" in a private room filled with toys that had been donated, along with wrapping paper, tape, ribbon, and a place to wrap them all. They also had Santa's snowy boot prints leading to each room as he delivered the presents on Christmas morning. That was such a special thing for the staff to have done.

Hearing the kids squeal when they opened their hospital-room door to see the footprints will be forever etched in my memory. For the kids, it was still magical, with lots of crafts, decorations, visitors—all the things. But for the parents, man, was that heartbreaking.

Seeing the children trying to be happy while in pain or feeling incredibly sick, while on chemo or with tubes coming out of them or while pulling their pumps in tow, or as they were wheeled around because they were so weak. Again, why was God allowing this to happen to these innocent little children? It just didn't seem fair.

Being in the hospital, especially during holidays, also puts things into perspective for you. Like a crash course in finding gratitude in all things. First, you realize just how lucky you are to be able to walk, talk, and be healthy. You find that sitting in traffic isn't a bother or pain in the ass; it is a privilege. You can now see that being able to work out, to go to work, to have to deal with crazy twins, to be busy with laundry and chauffeuring your kids around, and even to pay taxes is something that a lot of people will never get to experience and would gladly take on. There are people who are struggling with things I never knew existed and who would happily deal with all the things we think of as a struggle, instead of being in the hospital.

We were discharged again on New Year's Eve. Santa came to our house that night, and it's a good thing he did, because from January to March, we were in and out of the hospital several times. The toll taken on Ava's body by the severity of her pancreatitis really began to show. Plus, on top of the struggles from pancreatitis, Ava had suffered an injury during one of her procedures while she was sedated. Of course she did. That Laurencio luck struck again.

What I think happened was that someone tried to straighten her leg while she was under anesthesia and ended up tearing her hamstring. Her legs are incredibly tight, due to not doing a lot standing, walking, and movement. This led to peroneal nerve damage, which, by the looks of it, was excruciatingly painful for Ava. Poor peanut had been moaning in pain for weeks, and we all thought it was part of her healing from the pancreatitis. It was constant nerve pain that wasn't discovered until she had a foot drop, which is a clear sign of damage.

Once again, I cannot imagine her feeling that level of pain, constant, excruciating nerve pain, and not only not being able to tell anyone because she cannot speak, but not being able to ask for help to make that pain go away. While I know there was honestly no way for me to have known what had happened or suspect that it was her peroneal nerve, it still made me feel like a failure that I didn't. I had watched her suffer for weeks and didn't help her. That crushed me.

Add that on to the mental state I was already in, feeling emotionally beat up from all directions. Just like in the ICU, where I learned how to make something funny when I couldn't change it, I learned how to perfect my other coping skill–just move on. I would ignore it. Just file it away, push it down deep inside, thinking maybe, if I just pushed it down far enough, I wouldn't have to feel it or deal with it again.

At the time, it seemed like the best scenario, because it was truly the only thing I *could* do. I didn't have the mental capacity to deal with all that I had to, so something had to give. Before the pancreatitis, I had been living in survival mode, constant fight-or-flight, so I not only didn't have time to deal with these emotions, my body could not physically handle the emotions.

Plus, who could I really talk to about it? There wasn't a single person I knew who would ever understand how I felt or what I was going through. Not Manny, not Marjie, no one. So, for that reason, I found it easier to just internalize those feelings and wish for the best.

Unseen

There's a kind of loneliness that doesn't come from being alone. It comes from being the only one who truly knows the weight you carry.

I'd love to say that Ava's health stabilized and she's been working over the years on just maintaining it, but I cannot. Not only did I continue to have to put out medical-related fires for her year after year after year, but those fires were never easy to extinguish. Nor would they stay out. Also, as soon as one fire was put out, another one took its place. Wash, rinse, repeat.

Her pancreatitis and the complications from it caused so much damage to her body, she continued to struggle with healing for years to come. She went through several mysterious issues, like having red stones in her stool that tests showed should have been from her kidneys, but clearly were not.

How do I know that? Because I am lucky enough to have to give her a suppository daily and have been since she was about one and a half years old. In doing that, I have to hold her legs up for the "session," which can sometimes last over an hour. She struggles with the low muscle tone from her hypotonia, and her brain doesn't seem to send the message to push. That being said, I see the suppository go in, and then I see what comes out. And those red stones definitely came out of her butt.

Of course, I wanted them tested. Knowing where they came from wasn't enough. I wanted to know what they were and why they were there. Those were fun times, going through her poop, picking them out, cleaning them off, and putting them in a container to be tested. Wouldn't have been as bad if it was only once or twice, but no. Of course, not for us. I did this for months and months.

Another mysterious complication was she had an enlarged fatty liver and high liver enzymes. The side of her abdomen where her liver was visibly larger on the outside, and she also would rub it, which meant she felt discomfort. We took her to see several specialists, and no one could figure out what was causing it. We even took her to a liver specialist at Boston Children's Hospital for a second opinion, and even she couldn't figure it out. They suggested a liver biopsy, but My People were not on board for that.

Ava also started to have skin peeling on her hands and feet, along with issues with her toenails; ultimately, she ended up losing three of them a few times. She also started to have new types of seizures.

She developed severe sleep apnea, requiring oxygen at night. Since the pancreatitis episode, Ava had gained so much weight, she began to have oxygen drops overnight and ended up needing a BiPAP machine for sleep. She already was blessed to have a larger-than-normal tongue (insert sarcasm), and with her mysterious weight gain, the two didn't play nice together. She's a back sleeper, and the weight of her large tongue along with the weight gain caused her to struggle with breathing. She ended up being diagnosed with obstructive sleep apnea because of that.

My little peanut fought harder than ever to not use that BiPAP. She *hated* it. We tried every kind of mask they had, but it didn't matter. It was a hard no from her. Since sleep was the only time when she could truly escape from all the bullshit and pain she went through during the day, I decided I wasn't going to put her through that. If she didn't want to wear the BiPAP, then I wasn't going to make her. Period. Letting her sleep peacefully meant more to me than the potential risk. I have to pick my battles, and this was one that I was not willing to fight.

Her seizures also came back much stronger than before, and she had many episodes of status epilepticus (prolonged seizures over five minutes or repeated seizures without full recovery) for many years. Seizure episodes became pretty much a daily occurrence for her and lasted three hours or more, several times a day.

She also started to develop chronic hives all over her body. It looked as if she was covered in huge, blistery welts from head to toe. She'd wake up hive-free, and then they'd show up midmorning, become worse during the day, and then again die down overnight. No one knew why. We just kept throwing more medications at her as a Band-Aid, but no real root cause was ever found. That didn't sit well with me at all.

On top of all of that, she kept gaining weight. *A lot* of weight. It was baffling, because her diet had not changed at all. How was she up close to thirty pounds without additional calories, no more or less movement than usual, and no other changes to anything? It just couldn't be possible. Again, no one knew why, and no one was really chasing the cause. Just adjusting caloric intake to keep her from gaining. As with the other unsolved issues, this didn't sit right with me. It made no sense.

As her mother, watching her suffer through all of these seemingly unrelated but very bothersome issues was not only heartbreaking, it was incredibly frustrating. The solution, according to every specialist, was always to treat the symptom and not chase the root cause. The issues that arose were from different systems within her body (brain, skin, digestive, etc.), which meant different specialists. There wasn't one specialist who could oversee all of the things going on with Ava, so I really had to step up and be that person.

It was a big job for me to take on, for sure. There was barely enough brainpower for me to get through the day, being a stay-at-home mom to both Ava and the twins. But I needed to include time to research Ava's issues and try to find causes of each, plus also figure out how, though they seemed so different, they were somehow related.

Another thing that happened for Ava was, just a few years after her lengthy hospital stay, we got to experience our very first helicopter ride together. It was a medflight but so awesome, because hey, how many times do you get to ride in a helicopter? I was half scared out of my mind, because your kid has to be pretty sick to get to ride on one, but I was also pumped, because I'd always wanted to ride on one.

I remember joking, as my usual way of coping, to the pilot, while we were inflight to the other hospital. I told him how I always wanted to ride in a helicopter, but I thought my first time would be in Hawaii, not a scenic tour of northern New Hampshire at 3:00 a.m. As always, I was trying to laugh through the trauma. I couldn't change that, but I sure could laugh about it. I pushed the fear down deep inside and coped through humor.

We were put on the medflight because Ava needed to be transferred asap from the local hospital. She had RSV. Her breathing was extremely labored, and her oxygen very low. You are probably thinking, isn't RSV what babies get? Yup, it is. Ava's immune system is such a brat that, when she gets sick, she gets *sickkk*. What can be a runny nose for the rest of the family can end up being a helicopter ride into the ICU for two weeks for her. She was a teenager when she got RSV by the way. Crazy.

That unlocked in me a whole new fear. Now, I had to worry about every single sniffle the twins had. You have no idea how much stress that can cause. From the outside looking in, it seems like no big deal. When you live it day in and day out, though, it's exhausting. I had to constantly be on guard. Unless you experience this, you can truly have no idea. I used to be the person who practiced the five-second rule and thought kids needed to play in dirt and roll around on the floor to build strong immune systems. Now, I had to turn into the germaphobe who traveled with hand sanitizer, Lysol spray, and medical gloves in the car, avoided crowds, and all that immunity stuff. I hated it, still do. Remember how everyone acted during Covid? That is how I live my life every single day.

Speaking of Covid, when it hit back in 2020, I was freaking the F out. I was so happy when schools closed and switched to online. The next year, when the virtual option was offered at the twins' school for the entire school year, I jumped at that opportunity. For the next two years after that, I pulled the twins out of the public school and switched to homeschooling them. Did I want to? No. Did the twins want to be home? Also no. But unfortunately, it was necessary to protect Ava from potentially catching it.

It broke my heart to have the twins miss out on those years with their friends, but at the time, it was the right decision. Those were some hard years for all of us.

Ava did go through another month-long hospital stay after that. It was the summer of 2021. We went to the ER for a status epilepticus episode that I couldn't stop at home. She ended up getting diagnosed with a blood infection, which was a new one for her. What happened next was again something we hadn't gone through before.

She would not wake up. Like at all. Her body was acting as if she was in a coma. She never once opened her eyes for almost the entire month of August, and no one could figure out why. After a very long, stressful, and scary month with no answers and a whole lot of frustration, it was discovered that the medication they had prescribed to treat her blood infection in the ER was interacting with one of her seizure medications. It was causing the levels of that medication to multiply to toxic levels, which put her into a comatose state! Their error put my daughter into a drug-induced coma!

Don't get me started on how giving Ava the antibiotic and seizure medication red flag got missed by both the ER, the pharmacist, and the entire pediatric inpatient team at Tufts Children's Hospital in Boston, including their neurologist on call for weeks... When we once again transferred to our home away from home, the hospital in northern New Hampshire, their team figured it out. Her neurologist was shocked when he saw what her levels were and immediately switched her medications up. Within a week and a half, Ava finally opened her eyes.

Believe it or not, that hospital stay down in Boston was the hardest on me. This was on the tail end of the Covid pandemic, so everyone was still wearing masks, visits were limited, and Ava and I were completely alone. Since we were in Boston, we didn't get any visitors; Manny and the kids came maybe once a week to see us. Visits were not that long, either, because it was super-boring for the twins to be in the hospital. I mean, Ava was just sleeping the entire time. Mostly, it was so they could get hugs from me, give me new clothes, take my dirties, and return back home.

It was summer, so they preferred being home with Manny, enjoying the pool, playing outside, going to the beach, and eating ice cream. The twins also celebrated their tenth birthday during that hospital stay. While they did visit me and Ava on their special day, it was probably not what they wanted to do for first double-digit birthday. It broke my heart, once again, that Ava's unpredictable health ruined a special day for them. At least I got to hug and kiss them on their special day because they came down to Boston for a visit. That night, they FaceTimed me during the cake and ice cream time at their little birthday party with Manny.

I usually do well when I am in the hospital, but this one hit me particularly hard. I felt the most alone I had ever felt. I also felt sadder than I had felt in a very long time.

While once again I could not leave Ava, even if given the choice, I was so jealous of Manny and the twins. One thing about me is I *love* the summertime: I love the sun and love the heat. So, I was really affected by knowing they were enjoying probably one of the best summers of their lives, while I was stuck in a hospital room in downtown Boston, all alone.

I just sat at the window all day, looking down at the people in downtown Boston going about their days in the gorgeous weather. Life continued to go on, but not for us; certainly not for Ava, and not for me. I will never get back those four weeks of summer with my twins. I will never get back those four weeks of frustration, fear, exhaustion, etc. I was starting to realize I was always going to get the short end of the stick. I was always going to be the one who had to keep sacrificing.

But not only was it starting to bother me that I was missing out on things, I was also becoming pretty hurt about not being seen. I felt like my needs were invisible. I was feeling it was more, "Oh, Lisa will be okay. She always is." Or no one having to worry about anything, because, "Lisa will make sure it's taken care of."

Rather than, "Thank you for giving up everything for Ava," or "This must be so hard for you, to have to keep giving up everything you wanted in life for Ava," or "What can I do to help you?" Sounds a bit dramatic, but those are the thoughts that started to fill my head.

I sure as hell didn't want to spin myself into a depression, so I did what I do best: I pushed it down and filed it away. While this life was something I hadn't planned for and didn't even know existed, let alone want, it was now *my* life. I would no longer be able to make decisions in my life on what was best for me or for what I wanted. Ava's life decided all that for me. I couldn't make this situation funny, either. There was no joking to be had. So, down in the vault those feelings went, so I did not feel them anymore.

We did have one more ICU stay after that, but this time only for one week. It sounds so weird to say "only a week," but if you live this life, you catch yourself saying things like that more often than not. This particular ICU stay was in early 2025. Once again, because of Ava's pain-in-the-ass immune system, even though she is in her twenties now, when she caught influenza from her siblings, her body freaked out. Her grand mal seizures became super-violent, and at one point, she was having several per hour. She ended up with double-lung pneumonia and needed lots of help breathing and supervision in the ICU. She was on the edge of needing to be intubated the whole week.

I could go on and actually could write a book on just Ava's medical complications, but that would be pretty boring. Plus, I've already lived it once, so there is no need for me to go revisit it all by writing about it. It would destroy me. For that reason, let's just say what I've shared up to this point is only a taste of what we've been through. I've only written about the biggest issues Ava has braved, in order to help you to understand what has really been happening behind the scenes.

No one knew what was happening. No one knew how gravely ill Ava was at times. No one knew, because I didn't share. There was just too much. So, I internalized. I internalized because no one could help me, no one could help her, and no one could ever be able to relate or understand.

That internalization started to slowly cause me to fall apart, but I didn't notice. Honestly, no one did, because how could anyone notice when the Lisa they saw was always cracking jokes, smiling, and telling everyone she was "fine." She kept willingly taking on each traumatic event, pushing through, and making sure everyone was okay. Everyone, that is, except for me.

I had gotten so used to pushing everything down, so I did not feel or address my accumulating stress, loneliness, and unresolved trauma, that my instinct was to naturally push my feelings aside and file them away. I first started doing it so I could always be ready to handle the next medical crisis for Ava and stay focused on her. But even when there wasn't a crisis, I continued this behavior.

What I showed the world was that I was fine. I didn't share the fact that I hadn't slept one night through in decades, that I cried daily, that I was constantly overstimulated and jumpy, and that I was feeling completely unseen. I was lonely, and I felt invisible. I was emotionally and physically exhausted, always on edge, waiting for the next fire to put out, but I told no one. No one knew that I didn't like my life, and sometimes, I dreaded having to wake up again and do it all over.

I had no one to call.

I had no one to turn to.

I had no one to help me.

And I'd done that to myself.

It was all my fault, and I was getting what I deserved, or so I thought.

Before my mother passed away, she was my voice for me. She would be the one who would let the family know what was going on. I never had to call anyone, because she was so good at keeping everyone up to date. When she died, I should have stepped into that role, but I didn't.

I didn't really keep in touch with my friends, either, but they were another story. These were friends I'd had since high school, some from middle school. So, they knew me inside and out. We had so much fun over the years, and I loved watching them get married and start their own families. But most important, I loved being part of that. When it came my turn, I couldn't wait for my little ones to play with their kids and feel like I was part of the group again.

Except I didn't get to do that with Ava, because she was different. She also had those inconvenient immune issues, so being around a lot of people just wasn't safe for her. Or she would be having seizures or some other wacky medical reason to keep us from going to gatherings. Not only did I start to have to miss all of those fun things that I enjoyed so much—birthday parties, holiday gatherings, etc.— because of Ava's medical struggles, I started being invited to fewer and fewer events.

Since I usually said no or they knew it was something that Ava couldn't participate in, the invites started to slow down. While I would never throw shade on any of my friends, because I totally understand why the invites slowed down, it still hurt. They knew I'd most likely not be able to go or, if I did, I would not bring Ava, so we weren't invited.

What they didn't know was that I would have loved to go just to be with them. Oh, how I missed seeing them all. How I loved having people—actual adults, not just my kids, my husband, or Ava's doctors—to talk to. But again, how could they know? I never told them. Me, speak up about not getting invited? That would be considered a confrontation, and there was no way I wanted that. So, I stayed silent.

Because I was so focused on just surviving each crisis and, honestly, trying to get through each day, picking up the phone to call someone or text them wasn't really on my mind. Just the thought of it was exhausting. If I remembered, I'd make a Facebook status. But essentially, I was living, and am still living, in survival mode. And as you may have understood already, Ava can go from zero to one hundred in the snap of a finger. So much can happen in such a short amount of time, as I've mentioned before, if you aren't living it, it is very hard to understand. The thought of having to explain what was going on was even more exhausting to me than living through it, so I just kept quiet.

It felt to me like the times I reached out to update people, it backfired on me. Again, that is not their fault; it is truly all on me. But without knowing Ava's detailed history, all of the medical events I haven't shared, or even the physical, mental, and emotional suffering I've been through as her mother, witnessing all of these things, how could they empathize or react in any meaningful or helpful way? Their replies were the usual, "Praying for you," or "Let us know if we can do anything," or "You are so strong." While they truly meant well, those comments just destroyed me.

Why? For many reasons. First, those types of comments are often said to people whose kiddo broke their arm or to someone who lost their job or is going through a divorce, just as a few examples. While those people are absolutely going through a hardship and those comments are totally worthy and justified, I just felt like what Ava goes through and what I go through every single fucking day shouldn't be thrown into the same category or situation as people handling things they have chosen to have in their life, or that are fixable, or that they can eventually heal from and move on.

But how would people know that my situation was more severe, if I'd never told them?

That's what I mean by my sharing would backfire. I have been so silent for so long, just doing what needs to be done while falling apart behind closed doors, I think no one can begin to fathom my situation. So, they certainly had no idea that their genuine words of encouragement would end up making me feel even more alone than ever.

Remember how I described a new mother's trapped feelings with a newborn? How she constantly has to have her eyes on that baby and provide complete care for her baby, from eating to bathing to diapering to dressing, day and night? Remember how I said that raising Ava is just like that? Well, throw in all of the medical events, plus the phobias I've to live through each day, the life I had to give up, with the no days off for two decades, and then add in twins to the mix with their own issues. There are no vacations for me to "recharge." There are no getaways to escape to. There is no time off. There is no amount of sleep that can relieve the exhaustion that has become my norm.

I went off on a little tangent there, but you know what? I'm not going to edit it out, because, well, it's an honest expression of so many feelings I have pushed deep down inside.

So, let's get back to me explaining about how and why I have no one to turn to, and how it really is my own fault…

One thing about me is I will not ever crave attention for something that just needs to be done. Especially when it comes to my children. They were my choice to have, and anything and everything that happens with them is because of that choice. While I may talk about being stressed out, I will never, ever want to be "rescued" from something I am going through with them. I don't want to be put on a pedestal or seen as someone special. I am simply a mother who made a choice to have children, and I am doing everything a mother should do to care for them.

In the world of social media, I see so many mothers who are attention-seeking all the time. I see the "woe is me" mother posting about her child's hangnail and how she just can't figure out how to find time to get her manicure, go on her date night, or hang out on her weekend with the girls. I never want to be seen as that person, nor do I ever want to *be* that person. For that reason, I typically don't share about 98% of what it has been like with Ava and the twins. I wouldn't want the chance to be viewed as someone who is complaining or merely seeking attention.

So, when I get into situations where I need help or could use a friend's shoulder to cry on, I just don't reach out. It's kind of like trying to explain why a certain character is important in a movie when you have not seen any of the movie until the end. So much that has happened in the movie up to that point, there would be too much to explain for anyone to understand the true purpose of the character. Unless they've seen the movie from the beginning, there's no way they can grasp what is happening to that character or why they are important in the end.

I feel like that character.

I have internalized for so long that there is no way anyone could begin to relate to how I feel now or why I feel this way. And so, how could they console me or help me, if they can't relate or don't understand? I wouldn't want to put anyone in that situation either or make them feel uncomfortable, so I feel like I am shit out of luck.

I also I don't have a mom's group or support group or even know any families who have the diagnosis Ava has, because she doesn't have one! Sure, she has things that they have identified over the years, like cerebral folate deficiency, epilepsy, agenesis of the corpus callosum, and many more issues, but not one primary diagnosis. It is still not known what her primary diagnosis is or what is causing all of the things she has.

That means, even though she has those different diagnoses, the kids who share some of those same diagnoses are developing much differently than she is. As a result, I have no one who truly understands what it's like or who can relate to me, because there isn't anyone else out there like Ava.

Shit, even my own husband doesn't understand what I go through. Even around him, I internalize a lot. The times when he came to visit me in the hospital, the last thing I wanted to do was bombard him with all of the stress I was feeling from what I'd seen Ava going through, what I'd gone through, what I had heard being discussed about Ava, how tired I was, how lonely I was, and how depressed I felt. No, he doesn't need to deal with that, after working all day, driving three hours each time he visits us, and let us not forget, it's *his* child, too, in the hospital, so he has his own sadness and worries.

Back when my mom was alive, whenever Ava had any sort of medical crisis, she was the one who filled in my brothers and my dad on the details. She would talk to Manny about the emotional side of things, explaining how I was feeling, and she was the understanding, calming, and supportive ear I needed to listen to me and help me through. She would step in and take care of the smaller things in our lives, to help us out. Without her being the sort of "coordinator" who connected all of us, I have felt so far away from everyone. I have also felt so very alone.

Again, not wanting to ever be the one who wants any kind of attention, I kept quiet. I mean, Ava is *my* child. It is not anyone's problem or anyone's responsibility to keep me feeling seen or heard or cared for, when my issues are not something they can understand or, most of the time, even know about.

What I didn't realize about this method of coping, this method of keeping quiet and pushing things down, is that it has been the most damaging thing I could do to myself. I had no idea just how much harm I was doing, not only to my emotional state, but to me physically, as well, that would end up taking me years to heal.

So, I did what I've always done: I tried to fix it myself.

If I couldn't change the circumstances of my life, maybe I could at least change *me*. I couldn't keep pouring from an empty cup.

I began to look for something that would make me feel stronger, more in control, and more okay in a life that felt anything but. What I didn't know was that I was about to find a whole new way to disappear, disguised as healing.

Escaping

I wasn't trying to lose myself.
I was trying to find myself.
But somewhere along the way, the lines blurred.

Before I ever became a caregiver, before I was anyone's mother or even anyone's wife, I was a girl who loved going to the gym. I actually met my husband, at the gym. But, back then, I didn't go to the gym for health reasons or to get buff. It was more because I love to eat—a lot. I found, if I worked out and got a good sweat in, I could eat whatever I wanted and still rock a bikini. Like the best of both worlds! Plus, I am a hardcore people-watcher, and let me tell you, the gym is one of the best places for just that. IYKYK.

After getting married and then after having kids, fitness became more health-centered for me, of course. It also started to come last on the to do list after all the other needs of family and demands of life in general.

For me, I just didn't work out at all, because I wasn't able to physically *go* to the gym, and I could never stick to home workouts. I tried quite a few and didn't really like any of them. Plus, I didn't have the accountability provided by having people around me. I mean, how could I quit or give up, when people were watching? Ha-ha. In my living room, no one cared if I finished, so neither did I. Why bother?

After trying too many home workouts to count, I eventually stumbled on a home workout program that I fell in love with. It was the first one I completely committed to (and finished), and I got fantastic results. It was also the most challenging and the longest program I had ever done—ninety days.

I had never felt so accomplished as when I finished the last workout in those ninety days. I was so freaking proud of myself! Not only because I actually finished it, but because I could actually *see* the effort and commitment I'd made in my physical transformation—pretty awesome! I had never felt this before, and I immediately wanted everyone to be able to feel this way. It was too good to keep to myself. I wanted to tell the world about this program!

The biggest aspect that helped me to finish this program was that was the first time since having Ava when my effort actually matched my result. I had spent so many years trying to help Ava progress physically, working on her standing, kneeling, and arm strength. Also, I'd tried to help her progress mentally and spent my days searching the Internet for a diagnosis for her or to find a treatment that would help her. Year after year, I had absolutely nothing to show for the effort I put in. I even tried so very hard to get her to be able to eat and get over her trauma from those ugly earlier years of vomiting.

Nobody saw all of the effort I made behind closed doors, and for that reason, they had no idea how hard I worked for her, day after day. So, I was used to giving maximum effort with zero results.

So, when I found something that not only showed visible results from my efforts but made me feel amazing on the inside and look pretty darn good on the outside, *that* was just what I needed. Plus, it was something that was just for me. Lisa, not Ava's mom and not Manny's wife. I had found my new soulmate program.

After having Ava, I had no control over my life. But now, this fitness program gave me back some control. I not only felt stronger, but I felt lighter and more capable, and I finally felt my efforts actually *did* matter. I also felt like the Lisa who'd been silenced and buried under all of the stress, doing the caregiver role she was thrown into and the stay-at-home mom role she felt trapped in, was starting to show herself again. I welcomed her with open arms. Oh, how I wanted to feel like that Lisa again.

Fitness soothed something deep inside of me.

Deeper than I realized at the time.

What happened next was completely unexpected. Not only did I notice changes in my physical appearance, so did my friends and family. One day, when my brother stopped by to grab something out of my dad's garage, he said, "Damn, you got some pipes."

My brother is one of the reasons I first stepped foot into a gym. He has quite a history of sports, weight lifting, and powerlifting, so that compliment had me on Cloud 9! I was beyond flattered. My friends also noticed, and people started to ask what I was doing to get so fit.

I wanted them all to feel like I did, so of course I began telling them about the program and encouraged them to try it. They had to try it! I think I preached about it to everyone I came into contact with—ha-ha! I even bought a T-shirt from the program. When I wore it, more people asked me about it and I happily told them all about it.

I am not kidding when I say I told *everyone*. I sent so many people to the website to purchase that program and then couldn't wait to hear what they thought of it. I also offered to help with any questions they had and was more than willing to help them stick with it to attain the greatest reward at the end.

Shortly after completing the program a few more times, I got pregnant with the twins. Since it was a program that used some heavy weights, and since I was a high-risk pregnancy, I decided to not continue the program while pregnant. But I promised myself, after the twins were born, I'd get back to it as soon as I could. I may have been forty years old with newborn twins, but I was determined to get back into shape and even surpass the results I had the first time. I wanted to be a role model for other moms just like me. I could not wait to show them that, regardless of their situation or their age, they could do it. I also wanted to prove to myself that I could do it, too.

This was when I realized just how much joy and satisfaction I found in helping others have a chance to feel better. I had tried for many years to help myself or to help Ava, and I always came up empty-handed. No matter how much effort I put in, nothing could change the situation we were in. For that reason, I found it so incredibly rewarding to see how other people's lives were impacted by my efforts.

Plus, helping others was so much easier than trying to heal myself. When I could motivate them, guide them, and encourage them, I did not need to be as concerned about the shitshow of my own life. Seeing them succeed brought me genuine happiness and pushed my problems to be back. Still there, but hidden in the shadows.

Several years after the birth of the twins, I dusted off my workout program and did it again. I completed it several more times, and once again, because of my results, I found myself sending people to the site to buy it, when they wanted to "do what I was doing." That's when I realized the company had something called "coaches," who were doing exactly what I was doing, but they were getting paid for it.

For all the years I'd had the program, I was basically a coach–I just didn't know it, ha-ha. These coaches could earn a small commission off each sale of each program. So, for each person I had been sending to the website, I could have actually made an income from it. Blew my mind.

Could I do something like that? Could I do that with the life I had? Would I be taking on too much? Would I be able to handle it?

It was scary to commit to something no one else I knew was doing, but the thought of me being able to contribute to the family's income after over a decade of staying home was a pretty freaking amazing opportunity. I mean, I truly was doing everything a "coach" would do, so why not try to earn something? So, I signed up.

What I didn't know was, by signing up, it would open up a world for me I not only didn't know existed, but one I didn't know I could be part of. What I thought initially was just an opportunity to earn a little extra cash while helping women get healthy and fit alongside me soon opened up travel opportunities, friendships, rewards, bonuses, and a freedom I had no idea was possible.

All of that, along with still filling my cup with clients' success stories, made me feel seen, *really* seen, for the first time in forever. I was not only being rewarded by the women I was helping get healthier, I was being rewarded with bonuses, T-shirts, and trips, while being recognized by the best of the best. I was living an actual dream.

Looking back, I realize I wasn't just craving monetary success or all of the accolades from coaching. No, I was simply craving identity. Coaching filled the space where my sense of self had disappeared.

I went from the Lisa who wouldn't even leave Ava out of fear to go to the Walmart down the street, just five miles away from her, to the Lisa who went on planes by herself all around the world! Shit, I even went on a cruise! I remember looking out of my balcony on the cruise ship, floating away in the middle of the ocean, completely in awe of how far I had come.

Coaching gave me an incredible sense of belonging. It gave me amazing friendships, countless trips, the accountability I craved, and structure. I truly felt seen for the first time in many, many years. But, to be honest, I was not seen as my whole self. What people saw was the "positive, resilient, and strong" version of myself. The one who could overcome anything with a personal development quote, a healthy superfood shake, and a workout. The one who showed up every day to post her workout videos, who was always positive, and who continued to work her coaching business even when in the ICU with Ava. The one who truly could do it all.

The longer I coached, the more pressure I felt to keep up the version of myself people expected to see—someone who always finds the joy in every moment; the positivity spreader who works out every day, eats healthy, and loves every minute of it. There was no space to be exhausted, to want to skip my workout, or to lose myself in a pint of ice cream, be scared, or just be human.

The hidden part of me—who felt not good enough, exhausted, and still lonely—stayed hidden. They way I had found to keep that part of me hidden, even from myself, was to silence it. To numb it. To do that, I found alcohol.

So, while coaching gave me a freedom I had longed for, that freedom came with pressures I didn't know how to process. Alcohol made that pressure feel lighter. Alcohol allowed me to escape, relax, and let go.

When I was growing up, my mom was very against drinking. Up until the day she passed away, although I was a grown-ass adult and mother, I hid any and all drinking from her. If I wanted to have a beer on a random weeknight just because, she'd immediately act like I was an alcoholic. I'd get the look: that attitude and disapproval I mentioned before that I'd do anything and everything to avoid. So, I never drank at home. Ever. It just wasn't worth it.

When she passed away, I finally had the freedom to have a drink whenever I wanted. Manny had been having a glass of red wine nightly after dinner for his "heart health." I never had one with him, because if my mom had happened to come over and see me drinking it, I'd feel like I was in trouble. So, even though Manny offered me a glass time after time, I always said no, because I didn't want to deal with the implications of being found out. Once she was no longer here, I could join in and improve my "heart health," too.

Except, when I tried it, I almost gagged. It was nasty. Yuck. Not for me. I did, however, start looking forward to Manny and me having a few beers at the firepit in our backyard after the kids went to bed on Friday nights. Those Friday nights were something I looked forward to all week. I couldn't wait to just chill and feel the stress leave my body. It felt good to just let things go and escape for a bit.

I wasn't trying to escape my family.

I was trying to escape the heaviness I felt, which no one else could see.

What initially started out as one to two beers tops, just on Friday nights, jumped to three to four beers on Friday *and* Saturday nights. That soon turned into some weeknights, too. It eventually escalated to nightly, and I felt like I needed to drink more than I wanted to. The want was fading away and being replaced by the need.

It wasn't the taste of the beer I was after. It was the quiet it gave my mind. Alcohol quieted my thoughts in a way nothing else had been able to.

In the summer of 2015, I definitely recognized the addiction brewing and decided it was time to break this habit immediately and get sober. I have what people say is an "addictive personality." Basically, for me anyway, anything that makes me feel good or happy becomes something I crave. I struggled with an addiction to smoking and finally quit after two decades. I also have a history of disordered eating. Because of my history, I knew, if I didn't stop now, I might reach a point of no return.

I really wanted it to stick, so I tried an AA meeting. I was still anti-religious and a non-believer in God, so the AA meeting kind of rubbed me the wrong way, especially when all of the people at the meeting I went to were born-again Christians. It was very God-centered and just not for me. I decided instead to do it on my own.

A few months later, Ava went into the hospital with pancreatitis. So, by default, I *had* to stay sober during those months. I feel like God planned that one out for me, because I cannot imagine having to have withdrawals while living through that medical nightmare. Even though I didn't believe in Him, He was still looking out for me.

After all I went through during that lengthy and incredibly stressful stay, and the unthinkable and traumatic events I witnessed day after day, being alcohol-free was not something I wanted to continue once we were discharged. I convinced myself that I didn't have a problem and that I actually deserved to have a drink, if I wanted one.

I desperately needed a way to escape my life and calm my nervous system after all I had been through during the hospital stay. Ava was still very sick and I still had the twins to care for, so it's not like I could go anywhere for that escape. It felt like having a drink was the only thing I could do. Drinking seemed like the perfect fit.

Not wanting to get hooked on beer again, I thought I'd have that one glass of wine a night with Manny for my "heart health." Sure, I hated it, but it helped me to feel normal. It helped me feel more relaxed and, over time started to be something I looked forward to. It was my reward at the end of the day for all I had to do for the twins, for Ava, and for my coaching business.

Over time, that one glass of wine turned into two. I'd be on team Zoom calls with fellow coaches and drink my wine out of a regular glass, so no one would know it was wine. Even though other women were drinking wine during those calls, I was the only one who needed a refill, something I didn't want to be seen.

I also found myself sneaking to top off my glass if Manny left the room. I started adding ice to my glass, so I felt like I was drinking more than I was. I also found myself watching the clock every day for 6:00 p.m. to roll around. I thought, if I don't drink before 6:00, then I don't have a problem. I was under the impression that, to be an alcoholic, you were like the people in the movies—drinking all day, or having to sneak alcohol during the day. That wasn't me, so I couldn't have a problem, I thought.

Shame is a quiet, clever little bugger—it convinces you that hiding is safer than healing.

Still, every now and then, when I'd be having my "last refill" of the day, there would be a split second when something or someone would whisper in my head, "This isn't normal." I didn't want to hear it. I didn't want to believe it, and I certainly wasn't going to deal with it until after this glass was gone. I just wanted to feel numb.

Except I would find myself Googling symptoms of alcoholism, taking tests to see how I scored on the "Am I an alcoholic?" scale, and I even tried to cut back, which always made me drink more, not less. I'd search hashtags of sober people, of course while drunk, and want to feel like them so badly—with their genuine smiles and their bright eyes, always noticing their eyes were so alive. I wanted what they had so badly, but give up drinking to get it? Hell no. Not with *my* life.

Whenever I traveled with my coach friends, alcohol was the main event. Sure, we would go to trainings, go to group workouts, go to personal development seminars, and award ceremonies, but there was always alcohol (and tattoos!) involved. We were a bunch of moms from all over the country, gathered in a place far from our children and our husbands, enjoying a little fun and letting off a little steam. Of course, alcohol was involved.

At least that's what the other moms were doing. Me? I was trying to maximize every single minute I was away from home. Each time I went on a trip, I acted as if it was my last, because chances were super-high it would actually *be* my last. That meant I wanted to do all the things, drink all the drinks, and stay up until I was the last one awake. I did not want to miss one minute of anything. My drinking was excessive for sure, but I didn't necessarily stand out, since lots of moms were letting their hair down right alongside of me. And, well, they'd be feeling so good, they didn't notice just how much I drank.

How could I give that up? Coaching was what I found in order to do something that was rewarding physically and mentally. It brought me so much joy and created so much opportunity for me. Drinking, for me anyway, went hand in hand.

Going on those trips without alcohol would mean I would once again be limited to what I can do. That limitation is the hardest to accept as a mother to a special needs child. So, for me to finally find something that provided complete and total freedom? I would never want to give that up. Not being able to do anything longer than a few hours without packing all of the medical necessities, always watching the clock, missing out on so much in life due to illness and seizures… You know the drill. When I went on trips with these other coaches, these women, I felt limitless. I felt free. I felt like who I was before I had Ava and didn't know that the type of life I had even existed.

Taking away alcohol while living my freest life I had in years felt like, once again, I would lose control over something I loved. Sounds so dramatic, but that is how I thought.

In reality it wasn't losing control over something I loved. It was giving up control over something that was destroying me. I couldn't see it, because I didn't want to see it. My inner self knew that, once I gave up alcohol, I would have to face things I had pushed down over and over, year after year. I didn't want to.

What began as a "heart healthy" end-of-day reward in a glass turned into a tool I used for my survival. I drank not for permission to relax and take my mom hat off at the end of the day. I began to drink to silence my mind. To silence the thoughts, fears, and loneliness; the feeling not good enough, and the resentment. The fact that, even though I looked like I had it all together on the outside, on the inside, I still felt incredibly trapped in a life that, while I loved everyone in it, I just didn't want. I'd never signed up for this life, and alcohol let me escape from it.

Or so I thought.

I thought I could ignore the stress, push down the emotional trauma, outwork the exhaustion, and outdrink the parts of me I didn't want to face.

But silence has limits.

And my body was done being quiet.

The Undoing

This wasn't a breakdown.
It was everything I'd pushed down, rising back up.
My body wasn't failing me - it was forcing me to listen.

While the outside world only got to see the edited version of myself, this was not intentional. It was a learned behavior that I had developed over the years. I came from my method of coping and to prevent a total, complete breakdown.

I believed with my whole heart, if I pushed things down, if I sucked it up and moved on, if I silenced the anger, the frustration, the loneliness, and the fear, all of it, I could keep my head above water.

Just keep smiling.

Just keep looking for the positive in every situation.

And I did just that, for a while. But the daily responsibilities of it all not only didn't ease up, they intensified and continued to do so, as Ava grew older.

As the years and the decades passed, my grief at watching Ava's classmates and other kids her age continue to grow into adults never went away. They were becoming independent, with their own adult lives and careers, even starting their own families. It'd be impossible to not let that get to me while I was still stuck in the mode of providing complete care for Ava, who has remained developmentally unchanged for two decades.

I watched as friends of mine left the diaper stage then the terrible twos, the middle-school drama, the high-school angst, and for some they even became empty nesters. Me? I was still in the infancy stage with Ava and always will be. It's like being trapped in that movie, *Groundhog Day,* when every day is the same. Over and over and over.

I wasn't jealous of the other moms. I truly was happy for them. But seeing all of that and not getting to see Ava go through those stages left me feeling empty. Feeling like an outcast.

When I was blessed to be able to add the twins to our family, I knew it would open up a whole new level of exhaustion for me. That seemed worth it, though, because they would also give me a chance to enjoy what "could have been" with their big sister.

It was eye-opening just how much babies do on their own. Manny and I were both in complete awe of how automatic everything was for our twins. They cried when they were hungry, for diaper changes, or when they were tired. They could sit when we put them down, then learned to crawl, walk, talk, etc., all on their own. No help, no therapy, no pushing—they just did it all by themselves!

Even with two babies, I was blown away how easy it was! I didn't have to spend my entire day teaching them how to do things or trying to get them to hit milestones. It was automatic.

However, the twins did soon end up with their own issues.

Jillian started to experience anxiety in the early days of elementary school. It wasn't worrisome, but it was noticeable. I assumed it had been from all that she'd experienced, being Ava's sister. Both twins had been through so much, had seen so much, and had their lives affected immensely. So, for Jillian to experience some anxiety wasn't anything unexpected, and for that reason, I was not concerned.

That was, until third grade. Her anxiety attacks got more physically intense, with full-body trembling, and she would also get nauseous. For anyone who does not have emetophobia—something both Jillian and I suffer from immensely—the nausea would not be an issue. But for someone who freaks out around vomiting, having a panic attack that causes nausea brings it to a whole other level.

Her body would shake head to toe, with her heart pounding out of her chest; she'd be almost panting and totally unconsolable. She would get so worked up about her fear of vomiting, she would end up actually vomiting. That made her afraid of her panic attacks (how ironic…), because her brain thought they caused vomiting.

It got so bad, her brain became unable to tell the difference between being excited about something and being afraid. Because of that, her panic attacks started to affect her quality of life in a major way.

She went through years of intense anxiety and vomiting. She missed lots of school, got dismissed too many times to count, went in late a lot, missed birthday parties and class field trips, and even had to come home from sleepovers with friends. Not only did this break my heart, it was just another thing that kept my body in fight-or-flight mode. Her anxiety, since I knew what it could lead to, triggered *my* emetophobia and heightened *my* anxiety. But, being her mother, I had to try to hide mine in order to help her through hers. I had to push down my own fear, anxiety and suffering to be able to be there for Jillian.

It didn't end with Jillian's anxiety. Desmond has had his own struggles.

Desmond had a speech delay as a toddler, so we had a speech therapist come to the house for about a year or so. Both the speech therapist and the pediatrician continued to assure me that his speech delay was not uncommon for boys, and especially for him also being a twin. It was hard for me not to feel a little underlying panic, with his big sister having so many issues of her own. So, I did what I did best and kept my concerns to myself, pushing them down into the vault along with the rest of the things I wanted to forget.

Desmond did eventually start talking, just like they said, and soon was talking so much, we missed the silence—ha-ha. The worry-free period when he didn't have any potential issues didn't last too long, though. When he went to preschool, before I had to take him out due to Ava's pancreatitis, he started having pretty massive meltdowns. He would scream like he was getting attacked for four or five hours straight, no break, after I picked him up from preschool. This was the loudest, most constant, blood-curdling crying, like he was in severe pain. Again, I was told no need to worry. It was a phase, and he'd grow out of it, just like his speech delay.

I didn't worry too much, because honestly, I didn't have time to worry. I was just trying to stay sane during those days. His agonizing, hours-long crying lasted for years. And when the crying finally stopped, he began to show some behavior issues. We all thought it was because he had so much energy, he couldn't sit still in school. When I tell you this kid goes 100 mph from the moment his feet hit the floor in the morning until he lays his head on the pillow at night, I am not exaggerating. So, it made sense that he had a *lot* of energy to get out.

Except that wasn't it. Despite the tools at school and the plans put in place to help him, nothing worked. Also, at home, his defiance, dishonesty, and behavior continued to get worse, so I once again listened to my instinct. I knew something wasn't adding up.

Desmond has always been a love. Underneath his running around and craziness, he has such a kind soul. Because it wasn't adding up, I pushed the pediatrician for a referral to have him evaluated for a potential neurodivergent diagnosis.

Once again, my instinct was correct. I felt such relief, knowing something was causing the struggles we'd been going through all of these years. I also thought, after this understanding, things would get easier. They didn't.

I have received several calls from principals, assistant principals, guidance counselors, and teachers from two different schools because of his behavior. While I know he is such a lovable kid inside, he doesn't make the best decisions and often speaks without thinking things through.

All of this added to my stress and actually made me feel an intense amount of guilt. It had been my decision to bring these babies into this world, knowing they would have to deal with so much more than their peers. And while knowing that both of them had their own individual struggles was heartbreaking enough, adding the fact that I *had* to pay more attention to Ava and I *had* to jump when she needed me, it ate me up inside.

When I tried to view the situation from the twins' point of view, I didn't like what I saw. All I could see was a mother who put them second. I knew, in my heart, I was doing the best I could, but as kids, they couldn't see that. It made me want to fast forward to a time when they could understand why I hadn't been able to be there for them like I should. Since I can't do that, I just have to pray for their understanding.

While the issues with the twins paled in comparison to Ava's, they were equally draining and almost felt harder to deal with, as their mom. What I thought would be a walk in the park, parenting children who can walk, talk, and be independent, turned into a level of frustration and sadness I didn't know existed.

One of the biggest struggles about which I have been silent for many, many years is my marriage. I haven't talked about it or even hinted at it because, well, it's private. I also have felt it is something I should work on with Manny behind closed doors.

Choosing to be respectful and protective, however, has raised its own set of issues for me over the years. Just like with all of the other "issues" in my life, not talking about any of them and just trying to push them down and move on is not any real solution. It just creates more problems.

Since I have internalized everything and pulled away from many people over the years, I have lost all the friends who were close to me. I don't have a bestie or a friend group I can vent to or ask for advice. I didn't have my coach friends to talk to, either, because I did the same thing to them. None of them had lives like mine, so I stopped sharing the goings-on in my life. No one could relate to me. I was alone.

This has put me in a pickle for sure. But now, within the safety of this book, I am going to share a bit about those struggles, because I know other mothers in my situation have been suffering in silence. If my sharing will inspire just one mom to say, silently, "Me, too," then it will have been worth it.

Also, Manny told me he was cool with it—ha-ha.

Marriage is fucking hard. Even before we had Ava, Manny and I had struggles. Nothing major, but they were there. After having Ava, she became the priority, not our marriage. In the early days of her medical struggles, when I started to feel like I was not being seen, I began to pull away from Manny. Before I had Ava, I had already felt unseen, and that feeling magnified as the load I carried became heavier and heavier. I had my mom nearby, so she was my rock and my shoulder to cry on. She was my safe place, my go-to person.

What people don't know is, even though Manny and I were living together, there was an almost three-year period when we barely spoke to each other. We were just like two ships that passed in the night…

Like I said, marriage is hard, and marriage with kids is a whole lot harder. But marriage while trying to raise a special needs child with unpredictable medical needs? Let's just say the rate of divorce for special-needs parents is over eighty-percent. And the other twenty percent? I can guarantee you, half of those marriages are still intact because they have no choice.

I'd be lying if I didn't tell you both of us would have walked away and thrown in the towel numerous times. But out of our love for Ava and especially with me never wanting anyone else to care for Ava full-time other than myself, we have stayed together. And now, with the twins, there is a whole other reason to stay together, since we want them to grow up in a two-parent household. The life we give our kids has become more important than the life we are living. At least that's true for me.

You see, Manny and I can't do things to work on our marriage that "regular" couples can. We can't go on dates and haven't gone out more than a handful of times in Ava's twenty-two years. Ava requires an RN to be with her, and I will never leave her with anyone who doesn't know her, RN or not. Being nonverbal and having so many wacky issues and intense, life-threatening seizures, I always need someone who is familiar with all of her quirks and mannerisms, has seizure experience, and most importantly, someone who gets along with our family. That is harder to find than you think.

Also, for Ava's safety, she sleeps between us in our bed. That creates even more of a barrier and pushes us further away. Our relationship tends to involve us acting out our roles as individuals: he's the breadwinner and hard worker, and I'm the caregiver and stay-at-home mom. He does what he needs to do, and I do what I need to do. Our worlds don't mesh together like they would if we were able to spend quality time together. Even with the closest of relationships, that kind of structure, and after decades of the same patterns, can lead to a breakdown.

I have been hurting in every single area of my life. I felt trapped in my caregiver role, trapped in my marriage, and trapped in a never-ending head-butting relationship with my son. I even felt trapped in my daughter's anxiety, since I suffered along with her. While I will never find my excessive drinking acceptable, you can picture now why I used it as an escape.

A funny thing happened with alcohol, though. What I initially used as a means to *escape* my problems *became* the biggest problem. Rather than taking the edge off and making me feel relaxed, my alcohol use developed into something much, much darker.

I started to pass out on the couch every night. I'd wake up on the couch in the middle of the night or sometimes even not wake up until Manny got up for work. I'd still be sitting in the same place I was the night before, holding an empty glass of wine. Pretty sad.

I was in absolute hell. I went to bed hating myself, regretting things I'd said when under the influence, and I was so disappointed in my behavior as a mother. What a role model I was. It was completely irresponsible of me, as Ava's caregiver and keeper of all the medical knowledge, to drink so much. As the adult in charge of the twins and their safety. To drink myself to a blackout, nightly. I felt like I was so weak and such a failure for not being able to stop drinking so much.

After taking too many "Am I an alcoholic?" quizzes online, after watching every episode of *Intervention,* secretly wanting someone to set one up for me, and after scrolling Instagram to watch the lives of the sober community, I desperately wanted to be one of them. Then one day, I just decided the pain of staying the same was far greater than the pain of change. I knew, if I didn't stop then, I never would. And I knew that would eventually kill me.

I chose sobriety on March 7, 2020.

I didn't truly understand just how much damage I was doing to my body until I stopped drinking. I felt like total death and went through a detox I didn't see coming. I thought only heavy drinkers or people who drank the hard stuff went through detox symptoms from withdrawal. Um, hello, Lisa! Nightly blackouts *is* heavy drinking. The sweats, the nausea, the shakes, the dizziness, and the body aches after I stopped drinking opened my eyes to just how bad it had gotten and how far I had let it go. But I didn't have time to focus on myself for long.

On March 10, when I was just three days alcohol-free, Ava ended up in the ER again. And not just the regular ER, but in the trauma bay. She was having another one of her status epilepticus episodes, which was not new for her, but the fact that drugs were not stopping it was definitely new.

This trauma bay was not unfamiliar to me. It was the exact room my mom went in when she got taken away in an ambulance from our home. It was the room where I heard her voice for the last time. It was also the room where I saw her alive for the last time. Fun times.

The ER doc told me he'd given her enough drugs to take down a horse, but Ava's brain just kept on seizing. We ended up being transferred to the bigger hospital by a critical care ambulance. We came close to the medflight helicopter again, but it turned out the helicopter guys also do ground transport. In always looking for the positive, I have to say the ambulance was *nice*! It felt like riding in a limousine, and the driver was great to chat with for the long ride.

How could I expect my taking on such a major, life-changing event like sobriety to go any differently than that? Once again, I felt like whenever I take one step forward—in this case, a *huge* step forward, actually—life pushes me ten steps back. Words cannot come close to explaining the level of defeat I felt. Like why do I even bother to try.

I had thought that sobriety would quiet the chaos, but right out of the gate, it only got louder. And it only got worse from there on, because just a few weeks later, the world shut down for Covid.

So, there I was, trying to navigate my new sobriety and trying desperately to stay sober, trying to cope without my nightly escape or reward for making it through the day. And added to that, I now had the stress of the pandemic. The twins started virtual school, which was *not* easy. It meant, first, they were home all day, which meant they needed supervision to start with and hands-on supervision during the remote school hours. I was also dealing with Ava's increased seizures, plus her regular daily medical and caregiving needs, and doing it all alone, because, as usual, Manny had to work. *Ugh.*

I will always be extremely grateful that his job was not affected by the pandemic. He was able to provide for us without skipping a beat, but at the same time, I really felt the pressure of the extra burden I had to carry.

The pandemic also caused my home, the place where I should feel comfort, love, and support, to become a place I didn't want to be in anymore. I had no breaks, no breathing room, no silence, and nowhere to escape.

Even with that, when the school year was to begin again that fall, I chose the option of having the twins continue with virtual learning. As much as they wanted to physically go to school (as well as me and Ava did for our sanity, ha-ha), the safety of my children will always come first. For starters, at that time before any vaccinations or treatments were discussed, the virus was scary AF. Plus, there still wasn't much information on what would happen when kids got sick. I couldn't risk the chance of them catching it.

I also couldn't risk them bringing illness home, because I just knew with my whole being that Ava's immune system would not be able to handle the Covid virus.

Up to that point, 2020 had been a complete and total shitshow, with levels of stress I hadn't known were possible. But... it was also the year when I was turning fifty, and I could not wait to hit that milestone. My birthday at the end of the year, December 23, was definitely something to look forward to! I was so incredibly proud of myself for the person I was at fifty years old. I was fit, I was sober, and I felt and looked better physically than I had in a long time. Even with the craptastical life I'd been navigating, I never "let myself go."

For this big milestone of a birthday, I was hoping for and kind of expecting a day of pampering, appreciation, and being treated like the queen I am! Since we didn't have a nurse and even if we'd had one, not a lot was going on during Covid, so a surprise party definitely wasn't going to happen.

Since I'm being honest and letting it all out on these pages, I must say that's not *really* why there was no surprise party. The real reason was Manny never wanted to throw one. He didn't want to for any of my previous big birthdays, so my fiftieth would be no different. I was one of the last of my friends to hit our thirtieth birthday, because my birthday is so close to the end of the year. I went to all of their surprise birthday parties before my big day. Then, when my thirtieth came and went with no surprise party or anything special to mark the milestone, I was a little disappointed.

When my fortieth was approaching, I was very, very vocal about wanting a surprise party. I even told Manny, to make it easier on him and more cost-effective, too, I'd be open to a combo party with one of my friends who was turning forty just one month before me. Even with my own birthday, I was trying to figure out a way to make things easier for the other person.

You have no idea how flipping excited I was when I got an invitation for my friend's "Surprise 40th Party!" Duh, of course it was an invitation to just *her* party. But I just knew the other invitations that got mailed out to everyone else had both of our names on them. I couldn't believe the poker face Manny wore the whole time. He never slipped up, not one bit. He actually had me doubting there was going to be a party for me! He was very convincing about how he was not going to throw me a party, that he wasn't into that.

Our nurse was available to watch Ava that night, so we could go to my friend's surprise party together—of course she was! So, we went together. I actually got a little nervous when it was time to walk in. The only other time I had been surprised in my life was my bridal shower many years earlier.

But when I walked in, it wasn't what I had expected. The party really *was* just for my friend. The invitation wasn't a trick one after all, and Manny wasn't hiding anything from me. He had been telling me the truth all along. What a fool I was.

No party for me. I was crushed. It wasn't because I wanted gifts. It wasn't because I wanted to be the center of attention. No. I just wanted someone to go out of their way to make me feel special, because they thought I deserved it. And that didn't happen, even after I asked for it.

So, a fiftieth party definitely wasn't going to happen, pandemic or not. But… Manny knew how much I hurt about not feeling "special" on my other milestone birthdays, so I felt I was well overdue. Even without a party, he could still make me feel extra special entering my Fabulous Fifties era.

The day started out amazing! I woke up to 50 Cent "In Da Club" blasting in the kitchen. *LOVED* that! When I got to the kitchen, there were streamers and balloons hanging from the ceiling and a happy birthday sign. *OMG*, it was happening!!

Except that was it. The rest of the day was normal. Sure, we had cake and ice cream later, just like every other year. I got scratch tickets, like I did every other year. (I do ask for them, because I love Lottery scratch tickets—ha-ha.) But other than that, the rest of the day was like any other. Nothing out of the ordinary. No extra anything for turning fifty. Not even anything for celebrating my first birthday sober since I turned twenty-one. Nope.

I think it was then that I realized I truly could not rely on anyone else to bring me joy. I had to learn how to create some sort of happiness out of the chaos that was now my life. Me and only me. It wasn't Manny's responsibility to make me happy, so I shouldn't be upset when I felt like he came up short. He was doing what he was good at: providing for the family, keeping a roof over our head and food on the table, and allowing me to be able to stay home and raise our children. But being responsible for keeping me happy? No, that was all on me.

Next, I did what I do best. While trying to figure out what my next step was in life, rather than thinking of ways to help myself, I searched for ways to help others. I followed that feeling I had way back when Ava was a little bitty, that I was destined to be a voice for Ava's condition and to spread awareness to prevent other children, other mothers, and other families from going through what we did.

I was still doing the fitness coaching, though I had pulled back quite a bit. So, I thought, what could I do to stand out from the other coaches? How could I help them more effectively? How could I prove to people that my heart lies in actually helping women, not in building an MLM empire?

That's when I found out about the Holistic Health Certification program through IIN. It checked off all the boxes for me. I could actually not only take the class virtually, but when I graduated and got my certification, I could build a business that fit my situation.

I had hope again. I had excitement again. I had something to look forward to. I hadn't had anything to look forward to in such a long time. I once again was doing something no one I knew was doing, but it felt so right. The thought of helping women just like me to not feel what I had felt or hit rock bottom like I did, was amazing.

What I didn't know was that while fate led me to take that course and receive that certification, it wasn't to help other women. It was to help myself.

Once again, I had no idea how bad things were about to get.

Silent Damage

You can only silence things for so long.
The body always speaks eventually.
And mine was done being quiet.

I have always been aware of what stress can do to a body. I smoked for twenty years, so I knew my heart and lungs were already at a disadvantage. For that reason, I have been pretty good at paying attention to what hints or things my body would try to tell me. I've also been on alert for any signs of heart or cardiovascular issues because, well, I honestly have always felt heart problems are what my stress would cause.

But somewhere along the way, I stopped listening. I stopped paying attention to the subtle nudges my body gave me, letting my needs became more like background noise. I got too busy, focusing on Ava, raising my twins, and managing the household, so my body's cries for help weren't a priority. I could hear them, but I just wasn't paying attention to what it was trying to tell me.

I missed one of the first and biggest warnings that something dangerous was going on in my body. It was the first of many to come. Since I'd been expecting issues in my heart, I never really gave any thought to all of the other parts of the body that can get "sick" from the chronic and severe stress I'd experienced over the years.

It began with some really bizarre and achy nerve pain near my right shoulder blade. The first time I noticed it was at a hair appointment, as I lay back to have my hair shampooed. At the time, I had an undercut with bright pink and purple hair. Oh, how I loved that haircut!

When I went to my appointments, I was usually at the sink a few times during my appointment. I loved that time to lie back and chill, get my head scrubbed, close my eyes, and just savor that short period of pampering. *Aaah,* felt heavenly.

While I absolutely loved my hair appointments because they took a long time, the conversations with my stylist were always what I needed, and at the salon, I could be in the "real world" for a while. But, unfortunately, my trips to the salon started to cause me pain. The relaxing, feel-good moments at the sink became something I dreaded.

At first, we thought the bowl was too hard on my neck, so my stylist added a nice pillow for me. We tried adjusting the seat and the angle of the bowl, too, but nothing worked. The only way I could find relief was if I held my hand behind my back, twisted up behind my shoulder blades, while my head was in the bowl. Not so relaxing anymore.

I should have paid more attention to that and questioned why I was feeling it, but I didn't. I just chalked it up to having slept wrong or something simple like that. I should have done a little research on it like I always did for Ava, but I didn't. I should have run it by my doctor to see if something could be wrong, but I didn't. It had been so long since I made my own personal health or feelings a priority that those thoughts didn't even cross my mind.

The pain progressed from just the shampoo sink. It also started happening at home, too. I began to have pain when

I sat at my desk to work on my laptop for too long. So, I stopped sitting there and started to sit at our kitchen island or kitchen table, where I still had pain. I tried to stretch it out and change my position or use a heating pad to try to relieve the pain. Then, it even started to hurt just carrying my purse on my shoulder. Instead of wondering why, I simply switched to the crook of my arm, instead. When that started to hurt, I switched to a backpack purse.

My body was trying to tell me something was wrong, and I just wouldn't listen. I had gotten so used to shoving my own needs into silence, I didn't recognize when my body was done whispering and was beginning to scream.

That unforgettable scream came on a regular Sunday afternoon.

Sunday is my scheduled day to escape and by escape, I mean go food shopping. As I was driving home from grocery shopping, I drove past my house to get some surprise goodies for the family at Dunkin' Donuts. Extra half mile, extra two minutes. Not a big deal.

Except, as I got closer to Dunkin's, I started to feel really weird. Almost like I was going to have a panic attack. I felt off, like kind of lightheaded, with a bit of depersonalization going on. I kept driving, because, when I'd had this feeling in the past or started to have a panic attack, the best thing I can do is acknowledge it but just keep doing what I'm doing. So, I kept driving.

As I pulled into the parking lot, My People cut all the way to the front of the line and let me know something was wrong. Terribly wrong. Something was going to happen, and I needed to get *home.* I had such an overwhelming and sudden need to get out of there and back to my house. My People had never spoken up so strongly for *me* before, only for Ava. That sent real panic through my body, combined with an immense sense of dread. I immediately turned around to head home. I called Manny first and told him I wasn't feeling great and would be home in two minutes. I also told him I was scared.

As I made my way home, just a three-quarter-mile drive down the street to my house, I started to lose feeling in my legs and arms. My driveway was coming up fast, and I couldn't lift my foot off of the gas pedal.

My foot pressed harder.

The car was accelerating.

I couldn't stop it.

I was fully conscious but at the same time, trapped in a body that wasn't doing what I wanted it to.

Terror pulsed through my veins.

This wasn't anxiety.

This wasn't depersonalization.

This wasn't stress.

What the F was happening?

As I approached my house, I tried to turn the wheel with everything I had in me to get into the driveway, but I wasn't strong enough. I smashed into part of the stone wall at the edge of our yard and skidded into the driveway.

Somehow, the wheelchair van stopped. I don't remember how. But I was frozen. I couldn't move.

I couldn't feel my legs or my arms and thought maybe I was having a stroke or some sort of total breakdown. Manny came running down the driveway and pulled me from the car. He wrapped his arms around me to help get me into the house. My legs just weren't functioning right.

He sat me down in the living room in a chair, and we called Marjie and asked her to come as soon as she could.

Being the amazing woman she is, Marjie arrived within a half hour, so Manny could take me to the emergency room while she watched Ava and the twins.

While I sat in that chair waiting for Marjie to get to our house, my mind was racing, trying to make sense of what was happening. I was so afraid, but not of dying. No, I was afraid of losing control of my body permanently. If I couldn't move my body, how could I lift Ava? How could I be her caregiver? What would happen to her if something happened to *me*?

At the hospital, they told me: Not a stroke. Not a heart attack. No red flags. What? Something major clearly had happened. How was it not showing up on any tests?

They wanted me to have an MRI, but I'd have to get admitted, stay overnight, and have it done the next day. Since we were in the long process of paying off our already large hospital bills, I declined. Emergency rooms aren't cheap and this visit was already going to be a big addition to our existing balance. So, no thank you. I said I'd follow up with my primary care physician and get the imaging done on my own.

Oh, how I wish I'd stayed.

I followed up with my primary care doctor as promised. Even though the ER doctor was going to send over the records and MRI request, I kind of hoped she'd have more of an idea what had happened to me before I had to get the MRI. I thought she might have some answers, because I felt it should be obvious what was going on. That whole event was a pretty major blip in my otherwise "healthy body," I thought. To have no explanation as to why was just crazy to me.

Instead of getting answers from her, I got pure chaos and frustration.

She first blamed it on my thyroid.

My thyroid.

The same thyroid I'd been treating since 1999.

The ER labs showed that my TSH levels, though still in the normal range, had shifted out of "my" normal range. Was she kidding me? Anyone would know those symptoms could never be produced from a thyroid. Not to mention it's not like mine was untreated. I was diagnosed with Graves' disease, a severely overactive thyroid, and had it treated with radioactive iodine back in 1999. That treatment led me to a severely underactive thyroid. Once that bottomed out, I started taking synthetic thyroid hormone called levothyroxine, and I have been on it for almost thirty years now.

Because of all that, I've experienced every symptom of both an over- and underactive thyroid (except bulging eyes). None of what I felt at the moment was about my thyroid. Absolutely not. I told her this, and she insisted that I was wrong and her medical degree knew more about my body. I knew immediately in that moment she was not listening to me. She couldn't be. I was being treated like this was just some little event brought on by hormones.

What's next? I thought. Would she tell me I was dehydrated? That I just needed to drink more water?

Having been taught in Advocate 101 training as Ava's mother, I pushed back, which suddenly caused *me* to sound like the irrational one, questioning *her*.

I fought hard to get that damn MRI ordered, which the ER had said I *needed*. The one they were expecting me to get to help with a diagnosis. It should not have been an issue to order this MRI. Yet I pushed harder than I should have had to do, after crashing my car into a freakin' stone wall because my limbs suddenly stopped working.

She eventually did approve the order for the MRI. When the results came back in, she told me they found a lesion on my brain. Just one. But that was enough for her to confidently look me in the eye and tell me I had multiple sclerosis. She explained that the sudden loss of feeling in my arms and legs was from MS. She then referred me to a neurologist, so I could begin treatment for MS.

What the actual fuck? Multiple sclerosis? Absolutely *NOT*. I may have been through some craptastical events and Ava may have suffered through the unimaginable, but me getting MS was beyond cruel. I could *not* get a disease that takes away my movement, takes away my coordination, and takes away my strength. It was as if I'd been diagnosed with a terminal illness, because everything I would lose to that disease would end my life as I knew it.

I am so thankful she sent me to the neurologist she did. He was so kind. He listened to me and actually paid attention to the whole story, not just what the imaging showed. He told me my doctor should have never told me I have MS. It's not possible to diagnose someone with that from a single brain lesion. Also, I had no other symptoms other than the incident.

To investigate further, the neurologist ordered another MRI, this time only of my cervical spine. And that is where the answers came from.

The new MRI showed not only that I didn't have any lesions, but that the problem actually wasn't in my brain. It was in my neck. My C5/C6 disc was so damaged, it was compressing my spinal cord. So, off to the spinal surgeon I went for a consultation.

I lucked out with another fantastic and personable medical professional. The spinal surgeon, while he was a great listener and had great rapport, did not sugar coat things. I love that in a medical professional. He told me I was pretty much a walking time bomb and needed surgery immediately. He told me the reason I'd lost sensation in my limbs was because the disc in my neck had temporarily cut off flow in the spinal cord. I needed it fixed immediately, because I was at a huge risk for potential paralysis if, by chance, I got rear ended or even took a bad fall. Plus, what happened in my driveway could happen again at any time.

I flashed back to the warning signs I'd ignored. The pain at the shampoo sink. The pain when sitting. The loss of my ability to tip my head back. The pain putting my purse on my shoulder. I'd even ignored how my handwriting had been worsening. My body had been trying to tell me, and I hadn't listened.

Though I knew back and neck problems could potentially be an issue for me someday, I had ignored the years of wear and tear on my body. I'd continued to lift Ava throughout her entire life. I'd lifted her through my entire twin pregnancy, right up to a few hours before I delivered the babies, putting her in her wheelchair to go to the hospital with me. Sure, people offered to help, but I always declined. I figured I could do it by myself, so I did.

It turns out, just because you *can* do something doesn't mean you *should.*

A month after that appointment with the surgeon, in early 2020, I had an anterior cervical discectomy and fusion of my cervical spine.

I was so happy not only to have figured out what had happened and found a solution but then to be able to get it fixed. Crisis resolved, right?

Ha! If only. More like one down, many to go.

Sure, my neck was fixed. But my body was just beginning to show me what years of living in survival mode had done to me.

Unraveling

Surgery was supposed to fix me.
Instead, it exposed how broken I really was.

New spine, who dis? Actually, it was new spine, same shit.

I figured, once I had that spine surgery, I'd be good as new. Finally, something that was fixable and I could cross off the list. It was so rare to get closure on any medical issue, so this was a welcome change.

Except it didn't fix everything. It was only the beginning.

Up to that point, I thought I was doing enough to prevent spine issues by staying strong with fitness programs. I often preached about doing these workouts to help light that fire under special-needs moms, so they'd want to try the programs, too—to be strong for their own kiddos. So, for something like this to happen to me was not on my radar at all.

I was supposed to be the example, the person who showed everyone how to be and to stay strong. How was I supposed to continue to show up as the strong one when my body was starting to fail me? The unseen reality behind my apparent strength was starting to crack.

In the coming years, I ended up spending far too much time and money on physical therapy for recurring issues like these: recurring piriformis syndrome, recurring somatic dysfunction of pelvis, recurring somatic dysfunction of the sacral region, SI joint dysfunction, cervical spine issues—you name it. I also had countless X-rays, MRIs, CT scans, even ultrasounds.

What nobody noticed, especially me, was just how much pain and trauma this added stress had caused in my entire body. I had already been drowning under my daily chronic pain, then the surgery and recovery from that surgery, all while still caring for Ava and having the twins schooling at home. Oh yeah, and navigating it all while working on my sobriety and dealing with the craziness the pandemic caused. Next-level chaos.

I was frustrated. I was also pretty pissed off that my body was starting to fall apart physically when I thought I'd been doing everything right. I did exercise programs to make and keep my muscles and bones strong. *This wasn't supposed to happen to me.*

But, like everything else, I just pushed it down and sucked it up. As always, I ignored it and kept going. What choice did I have?

I had to use the little free time I had to pour myself into the Holistic Health Coach certification program I had committed to and already enrolled in. And honestly? That felt kind of exciting. It was a welcome distraction, for sure.

When I started the health coaching program, it was with the intention of helping others beyond just fitness. I wanted to learn how to help them as whole humans. Fitness is only a portion of someone's overall wellbeing, and I wanted to heal people's lives, not just through physical fitness. I knew from my own experience that fitness isn't a one-size-fits-all, and it is certainly not a one-size-"fix"-all.

This certification was just for me, for once. Not for the MLM I had aligned myself with for years. Not for Ava. Not for my family. Just for me. It was helping me see that, even in my situation, there was still something I could do to give myself more clarity on something that I had lost: *my identity*.

At the time, I had no idea that what had led me, subconsciously, to attain the certification actually had absolutely nothing to do with helping others. What I was about to learn, uncover, and implement became life-changing for me and for Ava. And ultimately, it would change the course of my life.

As I started going through the modules in the course, my eyes started opening to the brokenness in my own life and in my family's life. These modules taught me about stress responses, inflammation, gut health, nervous system regulation, nutrition, toxins, and more. They made me take a really close, hard look at my own body and forced me to face the reality that I wasn't well and hadn't been well for a very long time.

As women, we blow off so many of our daily "ailments." We are told they are due to hormones, lack of sleep, not drinking enough water, and the like. For me, I was also a mother, which in itself adds a level of stress that can cause more symptoms dismissed by the medical profession. Then, when you add in the higher level of stress for a mother of a special-needs child… You guessed it.

Diagnosis = super-stress

In my own particular case, I also have Graves' disease. I had an overactive thyroid that was treated with radioactive iodine way back in the '90s. While I take a daily medication that mimics a working thyroid, I am often told that some of my symptoms are linked to that treatment. Then, during my course, I was fifty-ish years old, so I was going through menopause and continued to have a highly stressful daily life. So, there seemed to always be something to blame my myriad aches, pains, and other symptoms on. It's just your thyroid or it's just menopause symptoms.

But as I continued doing the modules for my certification, I began to pay more attention to these so-called "inevitable" daily ailments of a typical aging woman, which I had been ignoring.

This started with sobriety. I had assumed, when I removed the bazillion carbs and calories in alcohol, which I was consuming right before going to bed, I would lose a noticeable amount of weight. I didn't. I did lose some, but not as much as I should have, after doing a 180 on my diet just by not drinking. What so many specialists and I had blamed on my thyroid and being over fifty was actually something else, and it would continue to make me feel worse over time, while being left untreated.

I was becoming more bloated each day, embarrassingly so. My stomach would swell up as if I was five to six months pregnant. I was eating clean, drinking tons of water, and exercising–it made no sense. I was also severely constipated and had migraine-level headaches every single morning as soon as I opened my eyes, I seemed to be racking up new food intolerances weekly, and was growing more and more exhausted. And I do not mean tired or sleepy. This was a level of exhaustion that no amount of sleep could ever fix.

Not that I did sleep. That was another issue—I hadn't had a full night's sleep in decades. No longer than three hours at a time. And when I did sleep, it wasn't deep, since Ava sleeps in the bed beside me. I am always on alert for a seizure. When I do fall asleep, it's always with me touching her arm or leg, so the feeling of her jerking from the seizure will wake me up.

Not to mention the many times I had to go to PT for pain in my neck, back, and hips. I'd go to different therapists for about eight weeks or so for each thing I thought was an "injury." My pain would subside after treatment, but then it would soon return again.

I just kept shrugging off all these developments as being due to my age, plus the wear and tear on my body from lifting Ava all of these years, added to the chronic stress of being a special-needs mom *and* a twin mom. Plus, all of that caused considerable emotional and mental stress, along with the physical. It was a vicious cycle.

But this holistic training course woke me up. I recognized that what I was experiencing was not normal. What I was feeling was my body sending me messages that something wasn't right. After all those years of pushing down all of the trauma, loneliness, anxiety, and fear, the jealousy, anger, and hopelessness, it now *had* to be dealt with. My body couldn't contain it safely any longer. And if I didn't both figure out what was going on *and* how to fix it, I just knew it wouldn't be pretty.

I started with my gut. Honestly, I hadn't noticed my constipation up until that point, but it was a major issue. That and my other gut problems all seemed to start after I got sober (or that's when I was aware enough to notice). I had assumed it was part of sobriety, but to be sure, I asked my PCP if she'd order a stool test for me. I'd heard a lot about candida and other GI/gut-health stuff, not only in my schooling but firsthand from people who had suffered from it. Rather than just order the test for me, she suggested instead I see a holistic gastroenterologist.

He ordered the stool test, along with a breath test to check for SIBO and some blood labs. What came back was equally shocking, eye-opening, and devastating. I wasn't feeling the way I was from my thyroid or from aging or menopause. It wasn't just me being a complainer. I was sick. *Very sick.*

He told me I had something he'd never seen before in his practice. I had grown so used to hearing the popular, "We've never seen that before," when Ava was the patient. But I didn't expect to hear it this time from my doctor.

I had SIBO, aka Small Intestinal Bacterial Overgrowth, but I didn't have just one type… I had all three of them. I had hydrogen-dominant, methane-dominant, and hydrogen-sulfide-dominant SIBO. In all of his years of practice, over forty years, my doctor told me he had never treated a patient with all three types. Nor had he seen someone as sick as I was. Lucky me. That good old Laurencio luck strikes again!

It didn't stop there, though. I also had adrenal fatigue, severe pancreatic enzyme deficiency, and my immune system was in the shitter. In a nutshell, my body was losing the fight to keep me going, and I'd had no idea.

He told me flat-out that I had to change. There was no more choice about it. If I continued at the rate I was going, I wouldn't ever be able to treat or heal effectively, and I would likely get worse. My body would break down more, and I'd be more susceptible to some big, scary things that a body can't fight, when it's not strong enough…

To heal was going to take a very long time, along with a major commitment from me. I was given a crazy number of supplements that were not cheap, to take three times a day. I think I averaged $400-$500 per month. I also had to go on a low-FODMAP, low-sulfur, low-histamine, and brassica-free (all the yummy cruciferous veggies like broccoli, cauliflower, etc.) diet. Which basically meant every single food I loved and ate every single day was off-limits.

And to reduce my stress. Sigh.

The next year and a half turned out to be the closest to living actual in hell as I have ever been. Dramatic, I know, but man, it was hard, and I was miserable! I had already given up alcohol as my reward and stress-reliever at the end of the day. After I got sober, I'd replaced that reward with nightly microwave popcorn and Diet Coke. The only reward I could safely give myself after sobriety was food. With the SIBO diagnosis, I had to stop all of that, too, for the most part.

I went through holidays without eating the delish holiday dinners with my family or any of the desserts and goodies that are such a big part of our holidays. I went through so many birthdays and birthday parties with no cake or ice cream. During the summer (my favorite season), I ate my bare-ass salad, while everyone else enjoyed all the cookout yummies. The hardest for me was no peanut butter, cream in my coffee, or smoothies. It was torture!

But I knew, if I took even one bite I wasn't supposed to, I could set myself back. This clean diet was designed to help me heal by starving the bacteria and decrease the stress on my gut. My gastro doctor was also very adamant about me reducing the stress in my day-to-day living. He actually told me he'd write a prescription for my husband to send me away to a hotel once a month to rest—ha-ha! If only.

Not only did I *not* decrease my stress during those eighteen months, it increased. There were more issues with my son, more anxiety with my younger daughter, and more seizures with Ava. There were even talks of spine surgery and brain implant surgery for her.

I did eventually kick SIBO out of my body, normalize my pancreatic enzymes, improve my adrenal fatigue, and heal my immune system. But one of the symptoms that still remained showed no change: my constipation.

One of the biggest lessons I have learned, being Ava's mother, is that the human body is not only designed incredibly well, but it is also not limited to whatever our medical textbooks say it can do. Each body is different, and therefore each body has its own unique aspects. Due to that, I've learned that even if a medical textbook says the body is generally supposed to react in a certain way, that is not always the case. I learned to question anything and everything.

One of the biggest lessons I learned from my Holistic Health Coaching certification course is that most doctors are trained in evidence-based medicine; they treat ailments, disease, and illness with medicine or surgical treatments. That is absolutely needed, and believe me, I owe Ava's life to Western medicine. However, they are not properly trained in nutrition (if at all), and, more importantly, they don't treat the person as a whole. Once I knew that, and as I became more and more frustrated by my own and Ava's accumulating issues over the years, when I was certified as a Holistic Health Coach, I became my own very-first client!

As my own coach, I was able to assess myself as a whole. What I eat matters. My stress level matters. My friendships matter. My marriage matters. It is *all* connected. Because of that, I was able to link together my recurring back pain, SI, piriformis, hip, tailbone, and constipation issues.

My GI, while wonderful, just wanted me to take meds for the constipation—a Band-Aid—and not keep searching for the root cause. So, I took it upon myself to research on my own and stumbled upon something called Pelvic Floor Dysfunction.

You'll never guess what I found. The answer I'd been looking for.

The newest official diagnosis for me is indeed pelvic floor dysfunction. I got testing at the hospital and then was referred to a pelvic floor specialist. Once again, after an evaluation with the pelvic floor specialist, I was told I was in pretty bad shape. She told me that from my head to my toes, I was exceptionally tight. It's like when you tense to protect yourself before an accident or when you tighten your core. Except mine was tense 24/7/365.

All those years of living in fight-or-flight mode had created a permanent tightness in my body. It had gone on for so long, my body got stuck and couldn't physically release. That tightness caused my whole digestive system to be screwed up, plus issues with my piriformis and SI joints, and putting my tailbone in painful spasms from the muscles pulling it so tightly. My back and my shoulders are tight and full of knots, and my thighs are a mess. All muscles, tendons, ligaments, and organs are too stiff and tight.

As I write this, I have been in PT for pelvic floor dysfunction for almost three months. I'm slowly making progress, but undoing years and years of constant fight-or-flight is going to take some time.

I wanted to include this in my book because so many women live their lives just like I have. You have stress, but you can't do anything about it, so you just keep pushing. You feel bad, complaining about your pain, or you don't want to bring attention to it, because how in the world will you find the time to fit in PT for *you*?

Maybe, right now, you're saying, "Holy shit, her symptoms sound just like me."

Good! I want you to learn to not stifle your feelings and not to ignore your body's warnings. I've learned the hard way the consequences of the "it is what it is" mentality. Please, be proactive with your health. Listen to your body. Don't be afraid to speak up, even if you are being quieted by medical professionals. It is *your* body, and you have every right to fight for it.

We, as mothers, but especially as special-needs mothers, have been on autopilot in order to put our children first and ourselves last. And while their needs certainly are top priority, our needs matter, too. We need to stop the mentality that self-care is somehow selfish. We need to stop thinking we'll deal with it later. *Later* may never come, if we let things go too far.

How good will our children be, if we aren't here?

It's time we stop pushing ourselves to the edge. But how?

I'm still learning how to do it myself, but I can say that I've made some good progress.

And the most eye-opening lesson so far?

Sometimes, the thing you keep pushing away… is the very thing you need.

Surrender

I kept thinking I needed to do more.
What I really needed to do was let go.

I often find myself going over a lot of the insane things I have been through with Ava, and I am just blown away that we are not only both still here, but we are both still standing. It's pretty remarkable, actually. We both still wake up every single day with a smile—it's a clean slate, a new chance to have a good day. It's always been pretty important for me to do this each morning, for both Ava and myself, although it's just Ava's nature to wake up happy. She has been a great teacher for me in that regard.

But then, I also find myself thinking about all the things we've been through in terms of how much abuse my body has been through because of it. Not just the physical abuse, but also the mental and spiritual trauma, too. Ava is and always will be the superstar and lead role in this story (ha-ha), but as a supporting actor, man, have I been put through the ringer.

I've often felt, the harder I try to heal from all of the damage that my body has endured through the years, the worse I end up feeling. I unfortunately still deal with a lot of the "same shit, different day" chaos twenty years later because Ava hasn't progressed mentally or physically. She has also accumulated more and more medical issues that require lots more care over time. These medical issues bring on a lot more worry and sometimes even unlock new, unknown fears.

For a body that is already taxed, that is quite damaging. Because of this, it kind of feels like I take one step forward in my healing journey, then I am forced to take ten steps back. For example, I'll start to feel some the benefits of my hard work and then another major medical event will happen or something else out of the norm will bring me all the way back to the starting line. Sometimes, even behind the starting line.

When I was in the trenches doing all of the hard work toward healing, just wanting to feel better, I wondered why I still felt so badly broken. Why did it seem like the harder I tried to heal, the *more* I was breaking? Or the sicker I felt or the sicker I became. Healing was supposed to make my life easier and help me to feel and be healthier. But it seemed, the more I tried to heal, the more was uncovered that needed to be fixed. Like my pelvic floor therapist said, it's like playing Whac-A-Mole. Best way to describe it!

Not only that, but the stress in my environment did *not* decrease. It just kept increasing as time went on. Talk about frustrating. Here I was, trying to fix all of the things that stress had caused, when I wasn't even the one—and still am not the one—who caused the stress!

It was also heartbreaking because I have always told my children that they should feel that our home is a safe place for them to be able to be comfortable being their true selves. Our home will always be a place for them where they can feel loved, heard, and accepted—no matter what. For some reason, even though it was such a priority for me provide a nurturing space for them where they would always be able to find comfort, rest, and love, it wasn't the same way for me. I was not feeling any of that in my own home.

I was surrounded by ongoing stress, crying out, and asking for help, but no one seemed to truly hear me and nothing ever changed. The amount of protection and care I had given to my family over the years was starting to cause my body to become sick. And unfortunately, everything I gave and gave to my family was not being reciprocated at all. Not even a little. That is such a deep feeling of hurt, words cannot explain it.

I could feel myself starting to slip mentally and head toward the darkness I had been in before: *depression*. While I didn't mention this earlier, I have been through two depressions. I'm not ashamed of that and certainly don't hide the fact from anyone that I have experienced depression. I just don't like to give any of my time to that part of my life. It's better to keep it in the past, as I believe it is not worth talking about.

I do, however, always keep myself on guard, fully aware that depression can come back at any time. When I feel that darkness lurking around, I speak up and am vocal to those around me. I want them aware, so they can keep an eye on me.

This time, however, when I could feel depression making its presence known, I didn't need to ask anyone to watch out for me, because someone else did. God did. Yup, the same God I had turned my back on. The God I'd thought was just a guy in the sky who was made up and didn't exist. It turns out, He'd been with me the whole time—I just didn't want to see Him. I didn't want to try to understand Him. I didn't want to believe.

I didn't have any major aha moment or all of a sudden burn all my secular music, stop swearing, and start to share the Gospel all day. It was more of a whisper from God. I felt led to start to pray every morning with gratitude and thanks, and every evening with the same thanks and gratitude. I started reading my Bible—alone. I didn't share it on social media, I didn't post pictures, and I haven't ever read it with anyone else. It was just for me.

I felt a strong pull to learn more about Jesus and His life. It was like I was being guided to learn. This was bizarre, since, again, I wasn't talking to anyone about this, and Manny never mentioned wanting to go to church or anything. It was just suddenly something I thought about daily and couldn't let go of.

I started seeing more and more content on my social media about Christianity. People sharing their stories of hope, love, and transformation. I admired their strength and longed for the clarity and love they had in their eyes. I wanted that so badly for myself. It was the same feeling I had when I was drinking and longed for the joy and pride that I saw in the eyes of those who got sober. I needed to feel that.

The more I immersed myself into rediscovering my faith, the more I saw how God had been in my story the entire time. God isn't something you chase or something that rewards you for a job well done. No. I learned more on my own personal journey of faith than in all of the years I spent during my younger life as a Catholic.

Throughout my life, when something bad has happened to me, I've thought, "Why is this happening to me?" If I am a good person, a giving person, an honest person, why does bad stuff keep happening to me? How come I see people who are not even the slightest bit kind get everything they want? Why do they get to experience all the joys of life, while I suffer over and over again?

That way of thinking is all wrong. When you are able to quiet yourself, quiet your mind, and truly have faith and believe in all that the Bible is and speaks of, you start to see things differently. Having something bad happen to me is not because I am being punished or because God doesn't see me or love me. He is preparing me. He is aligning me with the path He has chosen for me.

So, I instead of thinking, "Why are you doing this to me?" I think, "What are you trying to teach me?" All that I've been through and all that I've experienced have not happened *to* me. It has all been *for* me. Understanding that and trusting that it is all part of His plan and purpose for me, changes everything. Now I believe with all of my heart, if I did not have the opportunity to be Ava's mother, I would not be the woman I am today.

In going through the trials with Ava, I have been taught so many things about myself and my character, my strength, my love, even about the people around me. So, I wasn't being punished at all. I was being taught to prepare myself for what is next. For my plan and my purpose for being here.

I won't get too religious here, don't worry! But I feel this is important for me to share as part of my healing, whether you believe in Jesus, another God, source, or something else. No matter what you believe is your higher power, this still resonates.

Now, that doesn't mean bad shit won't continue to happen to good people. I know that firsthand. As a matter of fact, just earlier this year, in 2025, I was definitely tested.

The flu ran through our house, and for the first time in her life, Ava caught it. You recall the story about RSV, right? Because of that, I was freaking out big-time. If RSV, the illness that affects babies, put her on a med flight as a teenager, what would influenza do to her?

She seemed to be doing okay for almost a week, and I thought maybe her immune system had grown stronger and she was going to be fine. Nope. She tanked, and she tanked fast. Not only did she start having multiple back-to-back, very violent grand mal seizures, her temperature went over 104 and her oxygen was too low for us to maintain at home.

We ended up landing in the ER due to her oxygen needs. It turns out she had developed double-lung pneumonia. Well, shit. That's just one of the complications from the flu that can happen to people with weakened immune systems, so I'm glad that was all she ended up with. We were admitted and stayed in the ICU for a week.

That is stressful in itself, but it also just happened to fall during February school vacation for the twins, which meant they were home, alone. And once again, any possible fun or activities they had planned for their vacation went out the window. Also, once again, Ava took away something of theirs, which absolutely killed me. It just wasn't fair for the twins. But what could I do?

On top of that, Ava also had a previously scheduled seven-day inpatient hospital stay booked for the following week at the other hospital, up north. This appointment was for a continuous EEG (electroencephalogram that measures electrical activity in the brain like seizures), scheduled months before by her neurologist. The neurologist wanted this study done to gather information to help her figure out which kind of brain implant device would work best for Ava.

Just saying that sounds crazy, right? Brain implant device. Brain surgery. Anyway, it was just added stress, so I ended up having to reschedule the appointment when Ava needed to stay in the ER. There is no way her body would be healthy enough to bounce back that fast.

She made it through the pneumonia, and we were able to reschedule that EEG inpatient stay during, wait for it… April school vacation! I can't make this shit up. My twins are troopers for sure. Those poor kids.

While things still were and always will be crazy, life overall seemed more "stable" than it had been in a long time. While there were fires to put out and the stress was still high, it was at a more constant, even level of chronic stress. Not as many life-threatening stressful events; instead, just the continuous stress from Ava, coupled with the ongoing daily stress of raising a child with neurodivergent issues. That is a whole different kind of stress that, lots of times, feels quite intense.

Even with all of that filling my days, I started to feel incredibly lost, lonely, and less like a mother, more like a hired caregiver. I kept trying to find things to do that I liked but could also create joy in others and help them feel like more than being just a special-needs mom, a twin mom, or a wife. I kept trying to find joy for myself in outside, tangible things. I thought, if I could just do "xyz," then I would be happy. I kept looking outside of myself to heal my inner suffering.

I had always loved funny graphic T-shirts and had spent far too much money buying many of them. So, I thought, why not just make them myself? And so, I did just that—I started making them myself. I had hoped that selling my handmade T-shirt would bring as much joy to other moms as they did to me. Except, the more I did it, the more it just didn't feel right.

I also have always been a lover of jewelry, especially earrings—big, fun, festive earrings. For the same reason as with my T-shirts, I started to handmake those, too. I started with faux-leather earrings and then moved onto clay earrings. I made cute, holiday, and seasonally-themed earrings that made *me* super-happy when I wore them. I wanted to pass that happiness they gave me along to other moms. Except the more I did it, it just didn't feel right.

I just didn't feel comfortable trying to create joy for others when I stopped feeling it myself. Because of that, I closed down my website and shut my Etsy store. What I thought would help me feel seen and full or purpose now made me feel so much worse. I also felt embarrassed that people would think I was a failure, even though I had made the choice to close down. That led me to feel even more lost than before I started. I felt like maybe things weren't clicking for me because I was being selfish, by trying to divert my attention away from being caregiver and mom to other things. Maybe I truly was here only to be "just a mom." *Sigh.*

Even though I still felt detached from life and pretty down, I continued to show up and read my Bible every morning. I continued to try my best to put my trust in God's plan, but I felt myself starting to doubt His presence again. I know what I am going through is for me to learn, but what if I don't want to learn anymore? What if I am tired of the lessons and just want peace? What was all of this for? I didn't want to do it anymore. My bedtime started to include a sense of dread that I would have to get up the next day and do it all over again. I was tired. I wanted a way out.

That brings us to this past summer, the summer of 2025. One of my absolute favorite things about summer is my "pool time." I mentioned earlier in the book that summer and the sun are totally my jam. I feel like it heals me with its warm rays on my skin and feels like a cozy blanket. I love how it lights up the beautiful colors of nature.

Each sunny summer weekend, on Saturday and Sunday, I always try to shoot for one hour to float in the pool by myself, in silence. No one else, just me. I love to take in the sounds of the birds and feel the sun on my face, while being able to smell the flowers and grass around me. It is the most calming experience for me, and I will never, ever take it for granted.

On one of those days, I had another unexpected moment with Jesus. I was feeling so confused, so lost, and so upset. What was supposed to be my "me time" of floating, healing, and calming my soul turned into me crying and losing it.

As I looked up into the clear blue sky, I wondered if my prayers were being heard or if they were getting bumped for more severe requests. You know, moved to the back of the line. Trust me, I would be okay with that, but I just wanted to know that somebody could *see* me. That someone was looking out for *me*.

I kept asking of Jesus, "If you are doing all of this to strengthen me, why do I feel like I am getting weaker? What is it I am supposed to be doing? *Show me*! *SHOW ME!!*" With tears streaming down my face as I looked up into the beautiful, cloudless sky, I told Him, "I give up."

I meant it. I just couldn't do it anymore. I was tired of planning everything for everyone, trying to fix everything and everyone, and doing everything for everyone, even trying to find things that would help me be better and do better. My way just wasn't working any longer. I was truly at the end of my rope. I had nothing left to give. It was time. I told Him I was surrendering it all to Him at that moment.

I committed to letting Him lead the way and to learning not only to trust the path that was already laid out before me, but to embrace whatever was to come.

There was no strike of lightning, no rumble of thunder. Nothing happened. There was no instant change in me after that. Shit, I didn't even feel any different. Did He even hear me?

Why do so many people share their life-changing testimony after they have a surrender moment with Jesus following some major sign they couldn't ignore? Or how they changed immediately afterward? But not me? So many others have experienced such a profound personal moment in their faith after total surrender, while I, as usual, experienced nothing. *Ugh.* Again, I felt disappointed.

Most of all, I felt completely and totally unseen. Invisible. Unappreciated. Unloved. I felt like I didn't matter.

All of the feelings I had been trying to get away from all this time were consuming me. Now, the one I was supposed to turn to, the one I was supposed to trust in, the one who is the whole reason I was here wasn't even hearing me or acknowledging me.

Or so I thought.

Within the next week, I saw one of my old friends from my fitness coaching days mention in her Instagram story about writing a book. She'd talked about it before, and I thought that was such an incredible thing for her to do. Key word here was "*her.*" But seeing her describe writing a book and telling her story never once made me think, "Yeah, I want to do that."

I had never entertained the thought about writing a book. *Me*? Yeah, right. Let me just whip that up in my spare time. I had seen this woman post over the past year or so about how she now helps other people to tell their own story. *Good for them*, I'd think and just scroll past. Again, not for me. But that day, something changed in me. I didn't scroll past. Something bigger than myself made me stop.

I have been told over the years by many nurses, friends, therapists, and even people on social media that I should write a book because of the crazy stories I have around my life with Ava. But the thought of actually doing it was not in my wheelhouse at all.

But that day, when I saw that story about writing a book on Instagram, it made my heart start to race, pounding in my chest, and I felt a surge go throughout my entire body.

What the...? *Why? What is even happening to my body right now? Why do I feel like I need to message her?*

So, without even thinking twice, I messaged her to ask about it.

I'm sorry, *what did I just do? Who even am I, asking about a book?*

But honestly, I didn't think about it. I didn't hesitate. I just did it. I was led to this.

I think you know what happened next. How I got here is still a mystery to me, but I know for sure *who* got me here. It was nothing short of divine intervention that led me to put these words on these pages for you, for me. I didn't question it, I just trusted like I said I would, and here we are.

As I sit here, writing these words, I can see every piece of my story start to make perfect sense in a way I never thought it would. Writing this book was not an accident. It wasn't random. It was the beginning of something I didn't even know I needed.

I'd always put my heart behind trying to help prevent moms from struggling through what I did, by offering fitness programs and personal development. But maybe sharing my story in a way that those mothers could see themselves in it will be how the true healing begins.

And maybe, just maybe, it is how we can heal together.

Becoming

Becoming isn't about changing who I was.
It's about finally letting myself speak.

When I began the writing process, I was told—okay, I was warned! ha-ha—that I should expect the unexpected. People who had done this before me described it almost like opening a portal or raising a floodgate. Like unlocking a vault that they didn't even know was locked.

It was also suggested that maybe I should look into getting a therapist as I started to write, because of the rawness of the emotions I'd be letting out for the first time. I thought, *I'm fine.* I mean, I've been through a lot.

Within months of beginning to open up, uncovering feelings that had been suppressed for decades, and write everything down freely, guess who's in therapy? Didn't see that one coming, but it was very much needed. Oh, and not just for me. Also, marriage counseling.

Turns out, those warnings were right.

When I began putting words to the things I had lived through, I realized I'd never *processed* any of it. I just kept shoving every terrifying, traumatizing, overwhelming, and stressful moment down inside the deepest part of me and then moved on. That was my instinct, my natural coping strategy, and the only way I knew how to survive.

Silent survival.

The things I have feared most my entire life—being judged, being misunderstood, and letting it all out—have become the things I needed to truly begin to heal myself. Writing isn't just about me telling my story. It's me making peace with it.

Along with the therapy (which I should have done a long time ago), I also started searching for ways I could feel good in my body again. I had always loved fitness—remember, I met Manny in the gym back in what feels like a previous life now—but with all of my issues over the years, I eventually stopped working out. With my back pain, my cervical spine surgery, gut issues, and adrenal fatigue, fitness would have been more stressful than something to make me feel better.

Gyms were out for a few reasons. One, people—*ew*. Two, germs—again, *ew,* and I can't risk taking them home to Ava. Three, it was never guaranteed I could leave the house. I tried home yoga programs, and while they were okay, they weren't for *me*. While I felt great, I just didn't like it. The home programs I had done over the years previously were out, too, because they were much too intense for the phase I was in in my life. Plus, after years and years of doing them, it was time to move on.

Enter home Pilates.

Pilates challenges me without pissing my body off. It gets the job done without putting extra stress on my back, my hips, or my joints. And the instructor's voice? Oh, it is heavenly! Her cues are gentle and precise, and when I complete each of her workouts, I feel as if my body and my mind are finally able to *exhale*.

Because of that, I can see that what I initially thought were limitations—people, germs, and being stuck at home—weren't limitations at all. They were gentle redirections to lead me to something softer, something kinder, and something that works *with* my life, not against it.

Pilates started as a way to help my body feel better, but it turned into one of the missing links that led me back to myself. By calming my mind, by waking up my muscles, by learning to use my breath for healing, and by challenging myself physically without hurting my body, I found in Pilates greater meaning than I had realized.

It linked everything together for me. It showed me that all the experiences I have had were not random. Each and every one has been preparing me. They have all been happening *for* me, not *to* me after all!

But for what?

If everything truly happens for a reason, what is the reason?

Then, it hit me. The experiences, the struggles, the breaking down, the healing, the writing—all of *that* is the why I had been searching for.

The point isn't that I survived the storm.

The point is what I'm doing *with that survival.*

One of the main reasons I internalized everything and dealt with it alone was because I couldn't find anyone like me. Trust me, I have looked. Either other moms had things much worse to deal with than I did, which made me feel silly for saying I was struggling, or they had much less to deal with, so they wouldn't be able to understand how suffocating it feels to be me.

This caused me to develop the most unhealthy coping mechanism of all: *Silent Survival.*

I don't want any other mom to ever feel alone like I did.

Being strong has never meant staying silent. Venting isn't weakness. Wanting and craving connection isn't a luxury; it's survival. I was not meant to carry this alone, and neither are you.

If you are here, reading this book, we're in this together now.

I don't know what's coming next, but I do know one thing for sure: this book isn't the end. Writing has opened a door for me that I didn't even know existed. It has aligned me with the purpose I was put on this Earth to fulfill.

There is no turning back for me now.

The story on these pages has to end somewhere—but my becoming doesn't. I've survived so much in silence… and I don't want that for you.

If any part of my story felt like yours, walk with me.
There's more ahead, and I think you belong in it.

If you'd like to stay connected with Lisa, continue the conversation, or find support on your own caregiving journey, you can find her here:

www.LisaLaurencio.com
Instagram: @lisa.laurencio

Acknowledgments

Writing a book was never something I imagined I would do in my lifetime. But sometimes, life has a way of leading us where we're meant to go—not in the way we expect, but in the way we need.

This book exists because my story needed to be told and because someone, somewhere needed to see themselves in it.

I want to thank my publisher, SJ, for believing in my story and giving me the opportunity to tell it honestly. Thank you for creating space for this story to be shared in my own voice.

To my writing coach and friend, Raina, who helped me see my potential and helped me learn to see it for myself. Your encouragement and guidance made it possible for me to keep going during moments when I nearly lost the strength to continue.

To Marjie, who first came into my life as Ava's nurse but became my confidant, my friend, my family, and my safe place—thank you. You supported me through some of the darkest seasons of my life, and your presence has meant more than words can ever express.

To my twins, Desmond and Jillian, thank you for your patience, flexibility, and acceptance of a life that has asked more of you than it should have. Your understanding and compassion are beyond your years, and none of it has gone unnoticed.

And to Manny, thank you for continuing to provide for our family and for facing our challenges alongside us. That stability has mattered, especially during seasons marked by heaviness and uncertainty.

About the Author

Lisa Laurencio is a mother, caregiver, and advocate who has spent over two decades living the medical and emotional complexities of raising a severely disabled child. Through her lived experience and her pursuit of healing, she strives to remind others that they are not alone in their battles and their own well-being is worth fighting for, too.

By sharing the inner truths she kept buried, Lisa hopes to break the silence around caregiver trauma and the toll of chronic stress. Her deepest purpose is to transform the invisible weight caregivers carry into an understanding that offers comfort, connection, and, most importantly, hope.

www.ingramcontent.com/pod-product-compliance
Lightning Source LLC
LaVergne TN
LVHW090937080826
845145LV00003B/787

* 9 7 8 1 9 5 9 9 5 5 8 9 4 *